KIDS LOVE INDIANA

A PARENT'S GUIDE TO EXPLORING FUN PLACES IN INDIANA WITH CHILDREN. . .YEAR ROUND!

Kids Love Publications
7438 Sawmill Road #500
Columbus, OH 43235
www.kidslovepublications.com

02/03-12

Dedicated to the Families
of Indiana

ISBN# 09663457-8-9

KIDS ♥ INDIANA ™ Kids Love Publications

TABLE OF CONTENTS

General Information..…......Preface
(Here you'll find "How to Use This Book", maps, tour ideas, city listings, etc.)

(Amusements, Animals & Farms, Museums, Outdoors, State History,Tours, etc.)

Chapter Area Map

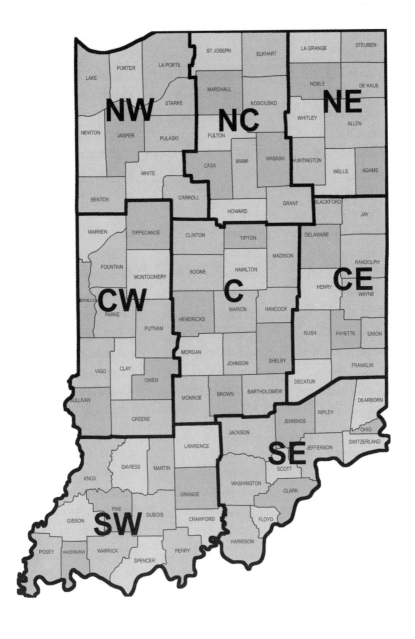

CITY INDEX *(Listed by City & Area)*

CITY INDEX *(Listed by City & Area)*

Acknowledgements

We are most thankful to be blessed with our parents, Barbara Darrall and George and Catherine Zavatsky who helped us every way they could – proofing, babysitting, and most importantly, inspiring family travel when we were children. They were great sounding boards and offered loving, unconditional support. Our own young kids, Jenny and Daniel, were delightful and fun children during all of our trips across the states.

We also want to express our thanks to Indiana Tourism, and many of the local CVB(s) staff for providing the attention to detail that helps to complete a project. We felt very welcome during our travels in Indiana and would be proud to call it home!

We both sincerely thank each other – our partnership has created a great "marriage of minds" with lots of exciting moments and laughs woven throughout. Above all, we praise the Lord for His many answered prayers and special blessings throughout the completion of this project.

We think that Indiana is a wonderful, friendly area of the country with more activities than you could imagine! Our sincere wish is that this book will help everyone "fall in love" with Indiana!

In a Hundred Years...
It will not matter. The size of my bank account...
The kind of house that I lived in... The kind of
car that I drove... But what will matter is...
That the world may be different
Because I was important in the life of a child.

- author unknown

HOW TO USE THIS BOOK

If you are excited about discovering Indiana, this is the book for you and your family! We've spent over a thousand hours doing all the scouting, collecting and compiling (*and most often visiting!*) so that you could spend less time searching and more time having fun.

Here are a few hints to make your adventures run smoothly:

- ❑ Consider the **child's age** before deciding to take a visit.
- ❑ Know **directions** and parking. Call ahead (or visit the company's website) if you have questions *and* bring this book. Also, don't forget your camera! *(please honor rules regarding use)*.
- ❑ **Estimate the duration** of the trip. Bring small surprises (favorite juice boxes) travel books, and toys.
- ❑ Call ahead for **reservations** or details, if necessary.
- ❑ Most listings are **closed major holidays** unless noted.
- ❑ Make a **family "treasure chest"**. Decorate a big box or use an old popcorn tin. Store memorabilia from a fun outing, journals, pictures, brochures and souvenirs. Once a year, look through the "treasure chest" and reminisce. "Kids Love Travel Memories!" is an excellent travel journal & scrapbook that your family can create. *(See your local book retailer or the order form in back of this book)*.
- ❑ Plan **picnics** along the way. Many Historical Society sites and state parks are scattered throughout Indiana. Allow time for a rural/scenic route to take advantage of these free picnic facilities.
- ❑ Some activities, especially tours, require **groups** of 10 or more. To participate, you may either ask to be part of another tour group or get a group together yourself (neighbors, friends, school organizations). If you arrange a group outing, most places offer discounts.
- ❑ For the latest updates corresponding to the pages in this book, visit our website: **www.kidslovepublications.com**.
- ❑ Each chapter represents an area of the state. Each listing is further identified by city, zip code, and place/event name. Our popular **Activity Index** in the back of the book **lists places by Activity Heading** (i.e. State History, Tours, Outdoors, Museums, etc.).

MISSION STATEMENT

At first glance, you may think that this is a book that just lists hundreds of places to travel. While it is true that we've invested thousands of hours of exhaustive research (*and drove over 3000 miles in Indiana*) to prepare this travel resource…just listing places to travel is <u>not</u> the mission statement of these projects.

As children, Michele and I were able to travel extensively throughout the United States. We consider these family times some of the greatest memories we cherish today. We, quite frankly, felt that most children had this opportunity to travel with their family as we did. However, as we became adults and started our own family, we found that this wasn't necessarily the case. We continually heard friends express several concerns when deciding how to spend "quality" and "quantity" family time. 1) What to do? 2) Where to do it? 3) How much will it cost? 4) How do I know that my kids will enjoy it?

Interestingly enough, as we compare our experiences with our families when we were kids, many of our fondest memories were not made at an expensive attraction, but rather when it was least expected.

It is our belief and mission statement that if you as a family will study and <u>use</u> the contained information <u>to create family memories</u>, these memories will grow a stronger, tighter family. Our ultimate mission statement is, that your children will develop a love and a passion for quality family experiences that they can pass to another generation of family travelers.

We thank you for purchasing this book, and we hope to see you on the road (*and hearing your travel stories!*) God bless your journeys and happy exploring!

George, Michele, Jenny & Daniel

GENERAL INFORMATION

ATHLETICS

❑ C – Bloomington. Indiana University Athletics.
(866) IUSPORTS or **www.iuhoosiers.com**.

❑ C – Indianapolis Tennis Center. IUPUI Campus. (317) 278-2100.
RCA Championships. US Tennis Association training site.

❑ C – Indianapolis. The Natatorium. Indiana University, 901 West
New York Street. (317) 274-3517. Three indoor pools of national
and international aquatic events.

❑ CE – Lafayette. Purdue University Athletics. (765) 494-3197 or
(800) 575-0285 or **www.purduesports.com**

❑ CE – Muncie, Ball State University. (765) 285-1474. Mid-
American Conference Division I-A.

❑ NC – University of Notre Dame. (574) 631-3000 or
http://ndu.fansonly.com.

BICYCLING

❑ Indiana Bicycle Coalition. (800) BIKE-110

❑ Hoosier Bikeway System. Department of Natural Resources.
(317) 232-4070.

CAMPING

❑ Hoosier Camper Guide. (800) 837-7842 or
www.campindiana.org

CANOEING

❑ Get Out & Go Guide. Tourism Division. (317) 232-4070.

❑ Liveries listings. **www.indianaoutfitters.com**

COUNTY PARKS & RECREATION DEPARTMENTS

❑ C - Hamilton County Department Of Parks & Recreation
(317) 896-3811.

❑ C - Indianapolis Parks & Recreation (317) 327-PARK.

❑ C - Monroe County Parks & Recreation (812) 349-2800.

❑ CE - Muncie/Delaware County Parks. (765) 747-4858.

- ❑ **CE** - Richmond Parks & Recreation (765) 983-7275.
- ❑ **CW** - Tippecanoe County Parks. (765) 463-2306.
- ❑ **NC** - Cass County Parks & Recreation (574) 753-2928.
- ❑ **NC** - Kokomo Parks & Recreation (317) 452-0063.
- ❑ **NC** – Kosciusko County/Warsaw. (574) 372-9554.
- ❑ **NC** – St. Joseph County Parks (South Bend). (574) 277-4828 or **www.sjcparks.org**.
- ❑ **NE** - Adams County Parks. (260) 724-2520
- ❑ **NE** - Fort Wayne Parks Department (260) 427-6000.
- ❑ **NW** - LaPorte County Parks. (219) 326-6808.

FALL COLOR

- ❑ Peak Fall Color Leaf Line. Department of Natural Resources. (317) 232-4002.

FARM MARKETS

- ❑ Indiana Farm Markets. Get Out & Go Guides. Office of Commissioner of Agriculture. (317) 232-8770.

FISH HATCHERY - STATE RUN

- ❑ **Statewide**
- ❑ Telephone Number: (317) 232-4080. Division of Fish and Wildlife.
- ❑ Hours: Monday - Friday, 8:00am-4:00pm
- ❑ Admission: Free
- ❑ Tours: By appointment
- ❑ Miscellaneous: Sites are Driftwood (Area SE), Avoca (Area SW), Cikana (Area C), Fawn River (Area NE), Twin Branch (Area NC), Mix Sawbah (Area NW), and Bass Lake (Area NW).

State run outdoor fish farms produce 200,000 to 1 million fish each year per site. Any of the six farms might raise trout, large mouth bass, blue gill, sunfish, and black crappie for stocking state parks. The caretakers usually start the tour with a slide show...then, it's out to the ponds. You'll be informed about the proper soil and depth of each pond and the vegetation that is most wanted. At the Avoca site, they have more than enough spring water from a cave nearby to supply their thirteen ponds. The best time to visit is harvest time when they drain the pond down to a minimum pool and wade through the water with a sieve to collect fish. In summer and early winter, the rainbow trout are easiest to see as they jump to the surface when you feed them.

HIKING

❑   Get Out & Go Guide. Tourism Division. (317) 232-4070.

HORSEBACK RIDING

❑   Get Out & Go Guide. Tourism Division. (317) 232-4070.

HUNTING & FISHING

❑   Division of Fish and Wildlife. (317) 232-4080.

RECREATION

❑   Indiana Recreation Guide. Department of Natural Resources. (800) 622-4931.

SNOWMOBILING

❑   Department of Natural Resources (317) 232-4070
❑   Indiana Snowmobile Association Hotline (574) 679-4006

STATE PARKS / RESERVOIRS

❑   (317) 232-4124 or (800) 622-4931 or **www.ai.org/dnr**

THE ARTS

❑   Indiana Arts Commission. (317) 232-1268
❑   Indiana Arts Council. (800) 965-Arts
❑   Arts Indiana Inc. (317) 686-2250

TOURISM

❑   Indiana Tourism (800) 289-6646 or **www.enjoyindiana.com.**

Check out these businesses / services in your area for tour ideas:

AIRPORTS

All children love to visit the airport! Why not take a tour and understand all the jobs it takes to run an airport. Tour the terminal, baggage claim, gates and security / currency exchange. Maybe you'll even get to board a plane.

ANIMAL SHELTERS

Great for the would-be pet owner. Not only will you see many cats and dogs available for adoption, but a guide will show you the clinic and explain the needs of a pet. Be prepared to have the children "fall in love" with one of the animals while they are there!

BANKS

Take a "behind the scenes" look at automated teller machines, bank vaults and drive-thru window chutes. You may want to take this tour and then open a savings account for your child.

ELECTRIC COMPANY / POWER PLANTS

Modern science has created many ways to generate electricity today, but what really goes on with the "flip of a switch". Because coal can be dirty, wear old, comfortable clothes. Coal furnaces heat water, which produces steam, that propels turbines, that drive generators, that make electricity.

FIRE STATIONS

Many Open Houses in October, Fire Prevention Month. Take a look into the life of the firefighters servicing your area and try on their gear. See where they hang out, sleep and eat. Hop aboard a real-life fire engine truck and learn fire safety too.

HOSPITALS

Some Children's Hospitals offer pre-surgery and general tours.

NEWSPAPERS

You'll be amazed at all the new technology. See monster printers and robotics. See samples in the layout department and maybe try to put together your own page. After seeing a newspaper made, most companies give you a free copy (dated that day) as your souvenir. National Newspaper Week is in October.

RESTAURANTS

PIZZA HUT & PAPA JOHNS

❑   Participating locations

Telephone the store manager. Best days are Monday, Tuesday and Wednesday mid-afternoon. Minimum of 10 people. Small charge per person. All children love pizza – especially when they can create their own! As the children tour the kitchen, they learn how to make a pizza, bake it, and then eat it. The admission charge generally includes lots of creatively make pizzas, beverage and coloring book.

KRISPY KREME DONUTS

❑   Participating locations

Get an "inside look" and learn the techniques that make these donuts some of our favorites! Watch the dough being made in "giant" mixers, being formed into donuts and taking a "trip" through the fryer. Seeing them being iced and topped with colorful sprinkles is always a favorite of the kids. Contact your local store manager for details.

MCDONALD'S RESTAURANTS

❏   Participating locations

What child doesn't love McDonald's food? This is your child's chance to go behind the counter and look at the machines that make all the fun food. You will be shown the freezer and it's alarm, the fryer and hamburger flipping on the grills. There is a free snack at the end of the tour. Telephone the store manager. They prefer Monday or Tuesday. Free.

SUPERMARKETS

Kids are fascinated to go behind the scenes of the same store where Mom and Dad shop. Usually you will see them grind meat, walk into large freezer rooms, watch cakes and bread bake and receive free samples along the way. Maybe you'll even get to pet a live lobster!

TV / RADIO STATIONS

Studios, newsrooms, Fox kids clubs. Why do weathermen never wear blue clothes on TV? What makes a "DJ's" voice sound so deep and smooth?

WATER TREATMENT PLANTS

A giant science experiment! You can watch seven stages of water treatment.   The favorite is usually the wall of bright buttons flashing as workers monitor the different processes.

U.S. MAIN POST OFFICES

Did you know Ben Franklin was the first Postmaster General (over 200 years ago)? Most interesting is the high-speed automated mail processing equipment. Learn how to address envelopes so they will be sent quicker (there are secrets). To make your tour more interesting, have your children write a letter to themselves and address it with colorful markers. Mail it earlier that day and they will stay interested trying to locate their letter in all the high-speed machinery.

COURT WATCHING

Call for an agenda of trials (docket info.) for the following: Common Pleas, Small Claims, Municipal, Domestic/Juvenile. See the Government Section or Community Services of your local White Pages. Did you know as citizens we have the right to enter a courtroom to observe (*except in special cases when a "Do Not Disturb" sign warns otherwise*)? Watching trials in session can be wonderful exposure to our legal system, especially for children who have studied law and government. Be sure your children have self-control before planning your visit.

Chapter 1
Central Area

Our Favorites...

Eiteljorg Museum

Conner Prairie

Indiana Museum

Indianapolis Motor Speedway

Mayberry Cafe

James Whitcomb Riley Old Home

Mathers Museum

HISTORICAL MILITARY ARMOR MUSEUM

2330 North Crystal Street

Anderson 46012

- ❑ Phone: (765) 649-TANK
- ❑ Hours: Tuesday, Thursday, Saturday 1:00-4:00pm
- ❑ Admission: General $3.00 (age 6+). Guided tours $4.50.
- ❑ Tours: Group Tours (for 10 or more) by appointment.

Walk among fully operational and light armor vehicles dating from World War II to Desert Storm. Note President Harry S. Truman's 1947 official Cadillac limousine or the Howe Fire Truck. The building is labeled the "Mess Hall".

ANDERSON FINE ARTS CENTER

32 West 10th Street

Anderson 46015

- ❑ Phone: (765) 649-1248, **Web: www.andersonart.org**
- ❑ Hours: Tuesday-Saturday 10:00am-5:00pm, Sundays 1:00-5:00pm.
- ❑ Admission: Small. Admission is FREE on Tuesdays and first Sundays.
- ❑ Tours: FRESH tour is $2.00 per person.

The lower level houses a children's hands-on gallery, display areas for temporary exhibitions of student and community art, and a classroom. The FRESH! Tour is of the Arts Center's permanent hands-on gallery for children ages four to twelve. Learn about color, texture, line and form while creating artworks and reproducing famous paintings such as the Mona Lisa and Arrangement in Gray and Black (ex. Whistler's Mother). Included in the ten activity stations are color mixing, spin art, sculptural puzzles, texture rubbings, and a silhouette booth.

ANDERSON SPEEDWAY

1311 Pendleton Avenue

Anderson 46016

❑ Phone: (765) 642-0206, **Web: www.andersonspeedway.com**
❑ Hours: Fridays Race at 7:30pm (May-August), Saturdays Race at 8:00pm (April-October).

Historic Anderson Speedway is home to weekly racing along with the annual Pay Less/Delco Remy America Little 500 Sprint Car Race and the Pay Less 400-Kendall Late Models. Admission.

ANDERSON SYMPHONY

Paramount Theatre, 1124 Meridian Street

Anderson 46016

❑ Phone: (765) 644-2111 or (888) 644-9490
   Web: www.andersonsymphony.org
❑ Admission: $15.00-$20.00 adult, $5.00-$20.00 child.
❑ Miscellaneous: For kids are concerts like Halloween and Christmas themes. The Historic theatre has playings of the old theatre organ occasionally, too.

TOM ST. CLAIR STUDIO GLASS WORKSHOP

6360 Pendleton Avenue

Anderson 46016

❑ Phone: (765) 642-7770,
❑ Hours: Monday-Saturday 10:00am-5:00pm. Call first. Occasionally, he isn't firing and closes shop.
❑ Admission: FREE
❑ Tours: Watch through large glass windows or pre-arrange a group tour.

Hand-shaped molten glass. He makes paper weights, ornaments, perfume bottles and sculpture that are multi-colored and have an "air brush" look to them.

MOUNDS STATE PARK

4306 Mounds Road (I-69 to CR 320 to CR 232)

Anderson 46017

❑ Phone: (765) 642-6627

Web: www.state.in.us/dnr/parklake/parks/mounds.html

❑ Admission: $3.00-$5.00 per vehicle.

The park features 10 distinct "earthworks" built by a group of prehistoric Indians known as the Adena-Hopewell people. The largest earthwork, the "Great Mound", is believed to have been constructed around 160 BC. It's a circular enclosure almost ¼ mile in circumference. Stand in the middle and catch the feeling of Ancient tribal ceremonies that might have been held. The nature center is located in the Bronnenberg House (open April-October), which is one of the oldest buildings in the County and was built from materials in the surrounding woods. Bridle Trails, Swimming / Pool.

MONROE LAKE STATE RESERVOIR

4850 South SR 446

Bloomington 47401

❑ Phone: (812) 837-9546

Web: www.in.gov/dnr/parklake/reservoirs/monroe.html

❑ Admission: $3.00-$5.00 per vehicle.

Scenic bluffs, rolling hills and lushly wooded areas surround Monroe Lake. Also features a Nature Center and Volleyball Courts, Boating, Camping, Fishing / Ice Fishing, Fourwinds Resort and Marina, Hiking Trails, Boat Rentals, and Swimming / 2 Beaches.

WONDERLAB

116 West 6th Street (between College and Walnut Sts., near Courthouse Square), **Bloomington** 47404

❑ Phone: (812) 337-1337, **Web: www.wonderlab.org**
❑ Hours: Tuesday & Thursday 2:00-5:00pm, Saturday 10:00am-5:00pm. Closed Thanksgiving, Christmas and New Years. Group tours available weekdays 9:00am-2:00pm by reservation.
❑ Admission: $2.75 per person (age 3+)

The Lab provides kid-friendly science experiments like Glues, Good Vibrations, Art Science, a Bubblefest, Food Science, Magic Secrets or Whirrers and Poppers. Each month WonderLab focuses on a different area of science, health and technology. Hands-on activities associated with the program theme change throughout the month. Check the calendar for special guest scientist programs.

INDIANA UNIVERSITY

107 S. Indiana Avenue

Bloomington 47405

❑ Phone: (812) 855-4848, **Web: www.indiana.edu**
❑ Miscellaneous: Stop by the Indiana Memorial Union (largest student union in the country) for a snack or shop in the bookstore. See separate listing for Mathers Museum located on campus.

Some attractions include:

❑ **MEMORIAL STADIUM / ATHLETIC COMPLEX** (1001 East 17th Street, 800-447-4648 or 812-855-9618 Stadium). The building houses the IU Department of Intercollegiate Athletics and is the home of the "Hoosiers". Of special interest are the trophy cases in the lobbies, the Athletic Hall of Fame, and the Olympic and NCAA , which hang in the arena. The public is welcome to tour the facilities between the hours of 8:00am-5:00pm, Monday-Friday. Please check-in with the receptionist at the football office complex under the east stands.

❏   <u>LABORATORY OF ARCHAEOLOGY</u> (423 North Fess Street at Ninth Street, 812-855-9544) . A major study and research facility in the field of Hoosier Archaeology. Included in the lab is a public museum devoted to Great Lakes/Ohio Valley archaeology and ethno-history. Hours: Tuesday-Friday 9:00am-4:30pm, Weekends, see exhibit through Mathers Museum. Free.

❏   <u>HILLTOP GARDEN AND NATURE CENTER</u> (2301 East Tenth Street, 812-855-2799). Access is the entrance drive to Tulip Tree Apartments off 10th Street. Home to one of America's oldest youth gardening programs, established in 1948. Greenhouses, ponds and perennials. Call for hours.

❏   <u>ART MUSEUM/LILLY LIBRARY</u> (Fine Arts Plaza, East Seventh Street, 812-855-5445). Ranked among the nation's best university art museums, the IU Art Museum holds more than 35,000 objects including paintings by such artists as Picasso and Monet. Artworks of the Western World from Byzantine to modern times, Asian and Ancient art, the art of Africa and the Pacific and the Pre-Columbian Americas are all at the museum. The building was designed by the world-renowned architectural firm, I.M. Pei and Partners. Hours: Tuesday-Saturday 10:00am-5:00pm, Sunday Noon-5:00pm. Free.

❏   <u>GREENHOUSE</u> (East Third Street, 812-855-7717). Located next to the I.U. Biology Department building, the Jordan Hall Greenhouse lets you stroll through green gardens, flowers and tropical jungles. It is a thriving greenhouse of unusual, exotic plants from every corner of the world. Individuals may tour during regular business hours. Group tours are available by appointment. Hours: Monday-Friday 8:00am-4:00pm, Saturday & Sunday 9:00am-3:00pm. Free.

❏   <u>KIRKWOOD OBSERVATORY</u> (Dunn Woods -East of Indiana Avenue, near Fourth Street). Built in 1900, the facility contains a 12-inch refractor telescope and other astronomical equipment. Viewing is available every clear Wednesday night when classes are in session.

MATHERS' MUSEUM

416 North Indiana Avenue (Northwest side of Indiana University)
Bloomington 47408

- ❑   Phone: (812) 855-MUSE
     Web: www.indiana.edu/~mathers/home.html
- ❑   Hours: Tuesday-Friday 9:00am-4:30pm, Saturday-Sunday 1:00-
     4:30pm. Closed during semester breaks.
- ❑   Admission: FREE
- ❑   Tours: Recommended. Guides bring the interactive displays to
     life. Call to schedule.
- ❑   Miscellaneous: Gift shop with items as low as $0.50. We'd
     recommend that each child purchase a different, unusual musical
     instrument to form a cultural band when they get home.

20,000 artifacts from across the world reveal traditions, values and
beliefs in objects people create and use every day. The kids hands-
on area has pretend houses in a European Village where you can
dress up and play house from different cultures. Check out
"Dancing the Ancestors: Carnival in South America" and "World
Music: Themes and Variations". After learning about and sampling
their huge ethnic instrument collection (our favorite part), ask the
guide for assistance in making one of your own using recycled
everyday materials. Unusual and exciting exhibits engage children
here!

MONROE COUNTY HISTORICAL MUSEUM

202 East Sixth Street (6th and Washington Sts.)
Bloomington 47408

- ❑   Phone: (812) 332-2517
     Web: www.kiva.net/~mchm/museum.htm
- ❑   Hours: Tuesday-Saturday 10:00am-4:00pm, Sundays 1:00-
     4:00pm.
- ❑   Admission: FREE, donations requested.

In the old, historic Carnegie Library is the county museum. The giant limestone pot gives you a visible landmark from the Washington Street entrance. "See Stories, Touch Time, Make Memories ! " is their motto. The Permanent Exhibits focus on the worker, education, entertainment, pioneers, and transportation in Monroe County.

BLOOMINGTON SPEEDWAY

5185 South Fairfax Road (3 miles south of town to Old SR 37 South, east at stop light on Fairfax Rd),

Bloomington 47426

❑   Phone: (812) 824-7400
    Web: www.bloomingtonspeedway.com
❑   Hours: Generally every other Friday (April-September). Pit Gate open at 4:30pm, Grandstand open at 5:30pm, Hot Laps 6:30pm, RACING 7:30pm.
❑   Admission: Average $10.00-$12.00, but may be more for special events. Children 12 and under are FREE.

The fastest quarter mile dirt oval track for sprint, open-wheel modified and street stocks.

CARMEL SYMPHONY ORCHESTRA

PO Box 761

Carmel 46032

❑   Phone: (317) 844-9717, **Web: www.carmelsymphony.org**
❑   Season: (September-May). Some outdoor performances during the summer.
❑   Admission: $6.00-$13.00.

Family concerts. Enjoy quality musical performances by talented local artists.

**WEST CLINTON
MENNONITE CHURCH**

ILLUSIONS - A MAGICAL THEME RESTAURANT

969 Keystone Way (Corner of Keystone & Carmel Dr. - Route 431)

Carmel 46032

- ❑ Phone: (317) 575-8312, **Web: www.illusionsrestaurant.com**
- ❑ Hours: Monday-Thursday 5:00-9:00pm, Friday and Saturday 4:30-9:30pm. Family Summer Magic Shows Saturdays 6:45 pm (Seating before 5:00 pm for Family shows). Reservations suggested.
- ❑ Miscellaneous: Average dinner between $16-$25.00.

The journey begins when you enter and have to remove the sword from the stone…and the giant wall magically opens. One of only 3 magical restaurants where the magic begins as your menu appears out of thin air. Enjoy excellent magic acts at your table after you eat. Be sure to buy a magic menu as your souvenir.

MUSEUM OF MINIATURE HOUSES

111 East Main Street (I-465 to Keystone, exit North, one block east of Rangeline), [US 431] to Main Street)

Carmel 46032

- ❑ Phone: (317) 575-9466, **Web: www.museumofminiatures.org**
- ❑ Hours: Wednesday-Saturday 11:00am-4:00pm, Sunday 1:00-4:00pm. Closed in early January and some holidays.
- ❑ Admission: $3.00 adult, $1.00 child (under 10)
- ❑ Miscellaneous: Gift Shop

"A world of small things awaits you". See antique and contemporary dollhouses, room boxes, and seasonal displays. Examples: the 1861 dollhouse, a large replica of a person's home; a 1/12th scale museum within the museum; a house all ready for the daughter's wedding and reception; and collections of unique mini accessories. Children can play the treasure-hunt game.

BARTHOLOMEW COUNTY HISTORICAL SOCIETY MUSEUM

524 Third Street

Columbus 47201

- ❑   Phone: (812) 372-3541, **Web: http://bchs.hsonline.com**
- ❑   Hours: Tuesday-Friday 9:00am-4:00pm and by appointment.
- ❑   Admission: FREE, donations accepted.

The museum is housed in the McEwen-Samuels-Marr home built in 1864. Permanent exhibits include a period bedroom and parlor and a pioneer exhibit from the early 1800's. Also featured are hands-on activity areas.

KIDSCOMMONS CHILDREN'S MUSEUM

4th & Washington Streets (The Commons Mall)

Columbus 47201

- ❑   Phone: (812) 378-3046, **Web: www.kidscommons.org**
- ❑   Hours: Thursday and Saturday 10:00am-5:00pm, Friday 10:00am-8:00pm, Sunday 1:00-5:00pm
- ❑   Admission: $2.00 general (age 2+). Children must be accompanied by caregiver.
- ❑   Miscellaneous: Large indoor children's playground in the mall.

The programs here are especially for children 2 to 12 emphasizing science, the visual arts, and community happenings. Activities vary monthly and might include an art-making station where kids may paint, create sculptures or self-portraits, or make inventions with "scrap" material from local industries. Toddlers may gravitate to the tunnels, building blocks and a soap bubble station where kids can see how big a bubble they can create and explore why they burst.

ZAHARAKO'S CONFECTIONARY

329 Washington Street (off I-65, downtown, across the street from
Commons Mall), **Columbus** 47201

❑   Phone: (812) 379-9329
     Web: www.inc.com/users/Zaharakos.html
❑   Hours: Monday-Thursday 10:00am-4:00pm, Friday-Saturday
     10:00am-5:00pm.

"Zaharaoplastion" is Greek for Confectionery. Zaharako's is
known for its turn of the century decor; a self-playing, German
pipe organ installed in 1908; two onyx soda fountains (once on
display at the St. Louis World's Fair) installed in 1905; Christmas
decorations; and the Cheese-Br-ger, Hot Fudge Sundae, and other
menu items. Fun names like "Fireball", "Double Up" or "Double
Down" are called out with many orders.

HENDRICKS COUNTY HISTORICAL MUSEUM

170 South Washington

Danville 46122

❑   Phone: (765) 745-9617
❑   Hours: Tuesday 9:00am-3:30pm and Saturday 1:00-4:00pm.
❑   Admission: Donations accepted.

Located in the former sheriff's residence and jail (1866-1974).
Visit and have your picture taken in "jailbird" attire. Also, see
items relating to domestic life, agriculture, military history and
education.

MAYBERRY CAFÉ

78 West Main Street (West of Indianapolis in Hendricks County)

Danville 46122

❑   Phone: (317) 745-4067
❑   Hours: Daily 11:00am-9:30pm or 10:00pm.
❑   Admission: Moderate pricing, home style food.

The trip into TV Land starts with Barney's Patrol Car parked out front! As soon as you walk in, you're transformed back to a diner cafe where home-cooked food is served. Many entrees are named after Andy, Opie, Barney, Emmett or maybe Floyd and desserts are Aunt Bea's (specialize in cobblers). Aunt Bea says, "If you finish your plate - you get dessert". Each child receives a token redeemable for one toy from Opie's Toy chest or one Opie Sundae. Andy Griffith reruns are played on TV's throughout the diner. Don't miss the autographed photos of the stars displayed throughout the site. Goober Hat Night is every Tuesday. Wear a hat and enter a drawing to win a free dinner.

CONNER PRAIRIE

13400 Allisonville Rd (NE of Indianapolis, I-465, exit 35 or I-69, exit 5)

Fishers 46038

❑   Phone: (317) 776-6006 or (800) 966-TOUR
    Web: www.connerprairie.org
❑   Hours: Tuesday-Saturday 9:30am-5:00pm, Sunday 11:00am-
    5:00pm (April-November). Closed Mondays, Easter,
    Thanksgiving, Christmas Eve & Day and New Years Eve and
    Day. EST
❑   Admission: $11.00 adult, $10.00 senior (65+), $7.00 child (5-12)
    (April-November). Half Price (December-March).
❑   Miscellaneous: 1823 William Conner House is a restored settler's
    and statesman's home - the finest in town. Tours every 20
    minutes for $1.50 additional charge. Museum Center exhibits,
    gift shop and Persimmons Restaurant (lunch/dinner).

Unlike many other historical villages in the Midwest, when you enter Prairietown, you really do interact as if you've been transported in time! All of the townspeople dress and act their character according to the year 1836. Mention of modern conveniences like pagers and cell phones is responded to with a blank stare. Your initial conversations may be a little awkward but you get the feel of things quickly. Pretend you're staying the night at the Golden Eagle Inn (for 12 ½ cents!) and then walk through town to visit neighbors like the Quaker printer, Jeremiah Hudson, or the Fentons (weavers - you can purchase yarn dyed naturally), or the Campbells (Dr. and Mrs. - definitely upper class). The kids' favorites were the baby lambs just born in the Conner Barn and the Schoolhouse. Sit on split log benches as the school master gives you lessons teaching the "loud" school method. Youngsters recite their different lessons aloud. Repetition is the key to learning and a ruler is used to discipline (not used on your first day of school, of course). Allow enough time to spend with chores like candle dipping, washing clothes on a washboard, spinning, gardening or by playing with 19th century toys in the yard.

JAMES WHITCOMB RILEY OLD HOME AND MUSEUM

250 West Main Street (I-70 to SR 9 to US 40, East of Indianapolis)

Greenfield 46140

❑   Phone: (317) 462-8539
     Web: www.greenfieldin.org/parks/rileyhouse.htm
❑   Hours: Tuesday-Saturday 10:00am-4:00pm, Sunday 1:00-4:00pm
     (April to mid-November).
❑   Admission: $3.00 adult, $1.00 child (6-17).
❑   Tours: Every half hour.

Mr. Riley was born in Greenfield in 1849 and his 1044 poems brought him the name, Hoosier Poet. (They are mostly about Indiana and kids). Famous characters he developed were the Raggedy Man, Little Orphan Annie and Old Aunt Mary from people he talked with and observed or events like the circus in town or a harvest festival. The best parts of the tour are the winding, creaky staircase, the rafter room, a cubby-hole and the chimney flue. Each spot plays a part in one of Riley's ghost stories. Little Orphan Annie used to tell stories that always ended "Er the Gobble-uns'll get you-ef you don't watch out!". Our guide recited several of these adapted, story poems with us throughout the tour - it was a delightful way to add mystique to a very simple home.

PRESIDENT BENJAMIN HARRISON HOME

1230 North Delaware Street (just north off I-65, downtown)

Indianapolis 46202

- ❑ Phone: (317) 631-1888, **Web: www.surf-ici.com/harrison/**
- ❑ Hours: Monday-Saturday 10:00am-3:30pm, Sunday 12:30-3:30pm. The museum is closed all major holidays, 500 Race Day, and the first three weeks in January.
- ❑ Admission: $5.50 adult, $4.50 senior, $2.50 student.
- ❑ Tours: Begin every 30 minutes, approximately 1 hour
- ❑ Miscellaneous: Gift Shop

See the 16 room Italianate Victorian home of the lawyer nominated for 23rd presidency in 1888. Stand on the front stoop where Benjamin Harrison gave 80 "front porch" speeches to 300,000 people who came by to listen. In the Master bedroom is displayed an old-fashioned home gym with weighted pulleys made from beautiful wood (a 19th century NordicTrack!) See the Library where election returns were tallied by telegraph. View a piece of Haviland White House china that Caroline Harrison designed choosing corn to surround the border because it was "a crop indigenous to the North American Continent". See creations of the First Lady, Caroline's paintings. Actual belongings of the Harrisons include an inaugural Bible, White House Tea Set and Parlor Sofa – but don't touch!

ATOMIC BOWL / ACTION BOWL

1105 Prospect (I-70 exit 83A or I-65 exit 111/Fletcher, turn right,
turn left on Virginia Ave)

Indianapolis 46203

- ❑ Phone: (317) 686-6006, **Web: www.fountainsquareindy.com**
- ❑ Hours: Monday-Thursday 11:00am-9:00pm, Friday-Saturday
  11:00am-Midnight-ish, Sunday Noon-5:00pm.
- ❑ Admission: $18.00 per hour per lane (up to 6 can bowl one lane).
  $2.50 shoe rental per pair.

Two Duckpin Bowling Alleys each represent a different period of
time. Action Bowl is on the 4th floor and has been restored to the
original time period of the building: the 1930's. Atomic Bowl is on
the basement level and has been restored to the 1950's era. The
Atomic features two juke boxes that play 45's with songs from the
period. There's also a Soda Fountain serving hand-dipped shakes,
malts, root beer floats, and ice cream sodas. Duckpin bowling is
very kid-friendly. The balls are just a little larger than softballs and
are easily handled, even by toddlers.

BALLET INTERNATIONALE

502 N. Capitol Avenue, Suite B (performances at Murat Centre)

Indianapolis 46204

- ❑ Phone: (317) 637-8979 or Box Office (317) 921-6444
  Web: www.balletinternationale.org
- ❑ Season: (September-April). Performances evenings at 7:00 or
  8:00pm, matinees at 2:00pm.
- ❑ Admission: $20.00-$60.00 adult, $20.00-$30.00 students (13-18),
  $10.00-$30.00 child (3-12).

Ballet Internationale is an ensemble offering a variety of full-
length fairy tale ballets, contemporary repertoire and an annual
production of The Nutcracker.

EITELJORG MUSEUM OF AMERICAN INDIAN AND WESTERN ART

500 West Washington Street (White River State Park)

Indianapolis 46204

❑   Phone: (317) 636-9378, **Web: www.eiteljorg.org**
❑   Hours: Tuesday-Saturday 10:00am-5:00pm, Sunday Noon-
      5:00pm. Open Mondays, Memorial Day through Labor Day.
      Closed Thanksgiving, Christmas Eve, Christmas and New Year's
      Day.
❑   Admission: $6.00 adult, $5.00 senior (65+), $3.00 child (5-17)
      and full-time students w/ID.
❑   Tours: Daily 1:00 pm
❑   Miscellaneous: Award-winning store offers authentic art,
      clothing, home décor. Many festivals held throughout the year.

Pottery, basketry, clothing, jewelry, paintings and sculpture of
Native American and Western artists. Kids Indian crafts or
demonstrations offered. Pick up the Family Guide listing of
activities and questions to answer. You'll feel you walked into a
Santa Fe courtyard as you tour the rooms.

INDIANA MUSEUM

202 North Alabama Street, White River State Park Museum
Complex (between Hall of Champions and Eiteljorg Museum)

Indianapolis 46204

❑   Phone: (317) 232-1637
❑   Hours: Monday-Saturday 9:00am-4:45pm, Sunday Noon-
      4:45pm.
❑   Admission: FREE, fee for some events.
❑   Miscellaneous: Gift shop with many Indiana-made items. Open
      beginning May 2002.

The interior exhibits include a three-story limestone quarry, a lock
from the Wabash-Erie canal, the reconstructed School 5 facade, an
art gallery, natural (early Indiana people and animals - geological

past with dinosaurs and glaciers) and cultural history (living history dramatic scenes, costumes) displays and the Foucault Pendulum, which is housed in the brick cylindrical tower. The Indiana Museum also contains a 250-seat auditorium and a 200-seat dining facility.

INDIANA PACERS

125 Pennsylvania Street (Conseco Fieldhouse)

Indianapolis 46204

❑   Phone: (317) 917-2100, **Web: www.nba.com/pacers/**

NBA Basketball. Boomer, the Panther is the team mascot and there's a fan club and kids pages/games on the website.

INDIANA SOLDIERS' AND SAILORS' MONUMENT/ COLONEL ELI LILLY CIVIL WAR MUSEUM

(Monument Circle - Meridian St, Center of Town... You can't miss it!)

Indianapolis 46204

❑   Phone: (317) 232-7615
      Web: www.state.in.us/iwm/civilwar/index.html
❑   Hours: Daily 11:00am-7:00pm. Access to Museum and Deck is
      more limited, call first if making special trip.
❑   Admission: FREE
❑   Tours: Observation deck open mid-April to mid-October.
❑   Miscellaneous: The USS Indianapolis Memorial, five blocks
      west, is of historical significance also.

Challenge your energetic kids to the 336 stair climb to glass-enclosed balcony at the top for a panoramic view. (An elevator is available up to last 45 stairs). See many bronze and limestone carvings (enormous and detailed) of famous Indianans like James Riley and President Harrison. The largest sculptures are of Civil Wartime Scenes. Throughout the year, the monument's steps play to performers, politicians and festivals. Inside the base is a museum with interesting city and war insights telling the personal stories of Hoosiers who fought to protect the Union and supported the Civil War effort. "Miss Indiana" tops the landmark with curved steps North and South and fountains with reflecting pools to the East and West.

INDIANA STATE CAPITOL BUILDING

200 West Washington Street (corner of Capitol Ave. and Washington St)

Indianapolis 46204

- ❑   Phone: (317) 232-9410 (when General Assembly is in session) . (317) 233-5293 (rest of year), **Web: www.in.gov/statehouse/tour**
- ❑   Hours: Monday-Friday 8:30am-4:30pm, excluding holidays.
- ❑   Admission: FREE
- ❑   Tours: Guided tours, 9:00 am-3:00 pm, every two hours. Self-guided tour booklets are always available at the Information Desk or in Room 220.

Built in 1882 (on the site of the 1835 State House) with Indiana limestone, the building contains executive, legislative, and judicial offices. There's a Rotunda in the middle with North, South, East,and West wings. See the Governor's office with the state-seal rug. Even some door knobs are embossed with the state seal - nice touch. Also, his desk is made from teak decking from the USS Indiana. Sit in on General Assembly State Supreme Court when in session (older, quiet kids only) beginning in January. Supreme Court matters tend to be dealing with serious, thought-provoking issues. Stories of things found during the last major renovation are engaging. The glass domes above are beautiful to look up at.

INDIANAPOLIS HORSE-DRAWN CARRIAGE RIDES

(Downtown), **Indianapolis** 46204

❑ Admission: Average $30.00-$35.00 per ride for up to 4 people on a 30 minute ride.

❑ Tours: Reservations accepted. Usually parked in front of major downtown hotels and Circle Centre Mall.
  - Circle City Carriages (317) 387-1516
  - Blue Ribbon Carriage Co. (317) 631-4169
  - Yellow Rose Carriage (317) 634-3400

INDIANAPOLIS SYMPHONY ORCHESTRA

45 Monument Circle (Hibert Circle Theatre)

Indianapolis 46204

❑ Phone: (317) 639-4300 or (800) 366-8457
  Web: www.indyorch.org

❑ Admission: $10-30.00 adult, $6-17.00 child (4-12)

Yuletide Celebration concerts, Family series, and Symphony on the Prairie Summer outdoor concerts.

MADAME C. J. WALKER THEATRE CENTER

617 Indiana Avenue (A few blocks from White River Park)

Indianapolis 46204

❑ Phone: (317) 236-2099

❑ Hours: Monday, Wednesday, Thursday, Friday 9:00am- 5:00pm, Tuesday 11:00am-5 :00pm

❑ Admission: FREE. Special events require a fee.

❑ Tours: By appointment. 30 minutes

❑ Miscellaneous: Asante Theatre programs for children (ages 8-18 years) to perform original plays centered on African American culture and current issues. Admission.

For updates visit our website: www.kidslovepublications.com

Because Madame Walker worked long hours and ate poorly, she began losing her hair. Frustrated, she cooked up different ingredients in her kitchen trying to find a solution that would make hair grow full and healthy. When she found a combination, neighbors began asking for some. Soon, she was advertising in newspapers and filling orders by mail. Madame created a line of shampoo, hair grower and oil treatments and began the first cosmetic direct sales. Known as the nation's 1st woman millionaire, the Center is a restoration of the former 1920's headquarters of her cosmetic business. Now it is a cultural showcase for the city's African American community. The theatre is decorated with African motif from collections of journeys to Africa. There is a small museum section in the Center that highlights artifacts from the entrepreneur's life and business.

PEEWINKLE'S PUPPET STUDIO

25 East Henry St, downtown (five blocks south of the Circle Centre)

Indianapolis 46204

❑   Phone: (317) 283-7144 or (800) 849-4853
      www.nashville-indiana.com/Attractions/puppet/show.html
❑   Admission: $5.00-$10.00 fee (free popcorn)

This old-world style intimate puppet theatre is complete with puppet gallery, 12' x 17' stage, full lighting, lobby and workshop capabilities. Puppets are available for sale. MMHP Puppet Productions present performances, field trips, workshops, birthdays and private events.

WHITE RIVER STATE PARK

801 West Washington Street (Downtown)

Indianapolis 46204

❑   Phone: (800) 665-9056 or (317) 233-2434
      Web: www.in.gov/dnr/parklake/parks/whiteriver.html

❏   Miscellaneous: Pedal boat and bicycle rentals.

You'll find trails, grassy areas, and waterways at White River State Park, just like you'd expect to see in any other state park. That, however is where the similarities end. White River State Park has cultural, educational and recreational attractions, too. A half mile Riverwalk Promenade made of Indiana limestone offers beautiful waterways, lots of grassy areas and tree-lined boulevards. The Pumphouse Visitors Center, IMAX 3D Theater, Eiteljorg Museum of American Indians and Western Art, The Indianapolis Zoo, NCAA Hall of Champions, Indiana Museum, Victory Field and The National Institute for Fitness and Sport are all within the park boundaries and offer some of the best cultural entertainment in the state.

INDIANAPOLIS ICE

1202 E. 38th Street (Indiana State Fairgrounds, Pepsi Coliseum or Conseco)

Indianapolis 46205

❏   Phone: (317) 925-4 ICE, **Web: www.indianapolisice.com**

The Indianapolis Ice hockey team, member of the CHL (Central Hockey League), plays 35 home games October through April. Be a Slapshot Kids Club member (12 and under) to join their special parties with players.

NCAA HALL OF CHAMPIONS

700 West Washington Street (One NCAA Plaza)

Indianapolis 46206

❏   Phone: (317) 917-6222 or (800) 735-6222
      Web: www.ncaa.org/hall_of_champions/global/home.htm
❏   Hours: Tuesday-Saturday 10:00am-5:00pm, Sunday Noon-
      5:00pm.
❏   Admission: $7.00 adult, $6.00 senior, $4.00 student (age 6+)

❑   Miscellaneous: Souvenir gift shop complete with exclusive
       NCAA merchandise.

The two-level Hall of Champions features four presentation
theaters, a 144-monitor video wall, numerous interactive and
hands-on displays, a turn-of-the-century gymnasium and a unique
view of the sports world via the "Look Up to Champions" video
display. From the "who, what and where" basics to our most recent
headlines, this is where they celebrate March Madness year-round.
The presentations in the Coaches' Locker Room and the Student-
Athletes' Classroom provide an insightful glimpse into the world of
college athletics.

INDIANAPOLIS CHILDREN'S CHOIR

4600 Sunset Avenue (Butler University)
Indianapolis 46208

❑   Phone: (317) 940-9640

Having grown to a program of over 1,200 singers in 12 choirs, the
Indianapolis Children's Choir continues to be one of the largest and
most accomplished children's choral programs in the nation. In
residence on the campus of Butler University, the choir makeup
reflects the diversity of central Indiana (singers come from 17
counties). In addition to its own concert series, the choir performs
regularly with professional symphony orchestras including the
Indianapolis Symphony Orchestra and has also performed with
The Chieftains and Celine Dion. The Indianapolis Children's Choir
has also performed several times at Carnegie Hall and regularly
tours both nationally and internationally.

INDIANAPOLIS CHILDREN'S MUSEUM

3000 North Meridian Street (30th Street between Meridian and
Illinois Streets - SR 37 North)
Indianapolis 46208

❑   Phone: (317) 334-3322, **Web: www.childrensmuseum.org**

Indianapolis Children's Museum (cont.)

- ❑ Hours: Monday-Sunday 10:00am-5:00pm (March-Labor Day). Closed Mondays rest of year. Closed Easter Day, Thanksgiving Day and Christmas Day.
- ❑ Admission: $8.00 adult, $7.00 senior (60+), $3.50 child (2-17). The museum is free for families the first Thursday of the month from 5:00-8:00pm. Cinedome admission add $4.50-$6.50.
- ❑ Miscellaneous: Annual passes available. IWERKS Cinedome - 3 story theatre makes you feel you're part of action - like being in a parade or hot air balloon. Dinosaurs, Indiana Jones archaeology dig, antique carousel.

Be sure that your kids have a good nap or plan multiple visits, because this place is full of 5 floors of fun! The well-known museum is as good as they say it is – a must visit! The largest and most popular children's museum in the world includes these favorite areas:

- ❑ THE LARGEST WATER CLOCK IN THE WORLD - Located at entrance & a marvel to watch-looks like a giant science fair project.
- ❑ PASSPORT TO THE WORLD - Cultures and people. Look through cutouts facing a mirror to see yourself dressed as a kid from another country or try your hand at playing foreign instruments or watching a performance.
- ❑ TRAINS: Locomotives "sight and sound" train depot really sound and feel like the train is leaving the station.
- ❑ PLAYSCAPE - Baby area with super soft play/crawl area and water, sand, garden, dress up, play house, areas for pre- schoolers.
- ❑ SPACE QUEST PLANETARIUM - 3 D flight and simulated star. Projection laser light shows to modern "hip" music and characters ("Garfield")
- ❑ EGYPTIAN TOMB - A 2700 year old real mummy with walk-along displays that teach you materials & scents used to prepare a body.
- ❑ SCIENCE WORKS - Send the pre-schoolers over to Playscape. School-aged children are hands-on with the Dock Shop multi-station water learning and construction site with stations where kids (using safe, scaled down material) pretend and play in all phases of constructing a new building.

INDIANAPOLIS JUNIOR CIVIC THEATRE

1200 West 38th Street

Indianapolis 46208

❑   Phone: (317) 924-6770. Box Office, (317) 923–4597
    Web: www.civictheatre.org/youthprog.html

1st – 8th   grade productions each season with its main stage
productions ranging from acclaimed musicals to comedies and
dramas. Productions might include Rumpelstiltskin, as well as The
Velveteen Rabbit, Winnie the Pooh and Charlotte's Web.

INDIANAPOLIS MUSEUM OF ART

1200 West 38th Street (38th and Michigan)

Indianapolis 46208

❑   Phone: (317) 920-2660, **Web: www.ima-art.org**
❑   Hours: Tuesday-Saturday 10:00am-5:00pm, Sunday Noon-
    5:00pm. Open late on Thursday. Closed Thanksgiving,
    Christmas, and New Years.
❑   Admission: FREE
❑   Tours: Daily at Noon and 2:00pm. Also, Thursday at 7:00pm.
❑   Miscellaneous: Snack area/café and Garden Terrace restaurant
    (Open for lunch only).

Known for Oriental art, "LOVE" prints and sculpture, African and
Indiana artists. Popular Family Days are a series of Sunday
afternoon events featuring self-guided tours, studio art-making
activities and related performances for families with children ages
5 to 10.

FORT HARRISON STATE PARK

5753 Glenn Road (Off I-465 & 56th Street)

Indianapolis 46216

❑   Phone: (317) 591-0904
   Web: www.in.gov/dnr/parklake/parks/ftharrison.html

The Fort - (317) 543-9592. Golf Resort and Harrison House Suites & 3 Officer's Homes, plus dining. Landscape and history are blended in a unique setting at the 1700-acre park featuring walking and jogging trails, picnic sites, fishing access to Fall Creek and two national historic districts. The former Citizen's Military Training Camp, Civilian Conservation Corps camp, and World War II prisoner of war camp is preserved at the park headquarters location. Many plan hikes after visiting the interpretive center exhibits and talking with park naturalists. Others go bird watching for woodpeckers and warblers amongst the wildflowers in the forest. Bridle/biking trails and fishing are here, too.

INDIANA STATE POLICE YOUTH EDUCATION AND HISTORICAL CENTER

8500 East 21st Street (Off 1-70, east of downtown)

Indianapolis 46219

❑   Phone: (317) 899-8293,
❑   Hours: Monday-Friday 8:00am-Noon and 1:00-4:00pm
❑   Admission: Donation
❑   Tours: Groups by appointment.

To teach respect for the police force or to pretend to be an officer for awhile – here's the place to go. Police vehicles are everywhere - restored classics, miniature police cars from every state or you can sit in a real car (turn on lights, sirens or intercom radio). Also, see displays and firearms; exhibit of Indiana's own John Dillinger; or bicycle safety.

INDIANAPOLIS MOTOR SPEEDWAY

4790 West 16th Street

Indianapolis 46222

- ❑ Phone: (317) 484-6784, **Web: www.indy500.com/museum**
- ❑ Hours: Daily 9:00am-5:00pm (except Christmas Day)
- ❑ Admission: General Admission $1-3.00 track tour, $1-3.00 museum (ages 6 and under free).
- ❑ Tours: By mini-bus, weather permitting.
- ❑ Miscellaneous: Gift shop. Home of the Indy 500 and the NASCAR Brickyard 400.

Drive right onto the inside track as you are awed by the size of the speedway. Built initially as a proving ground for autos, it developed into the largest one day sporting event in the world and the greatest spectacle in racing – the Indy 500. The Hall of Fame Museum contains over 75 vehicles and numerous artifacts and trivia videos. Antique motorized vehicles, race winning cars, pace cars and even a rocket – boosted car can be seen. Stop in the theatre to view a film of race highlights. Maybe the best part of your visit will be the racetrack bus tour. Adrenaline is pumping as you make one lap with a narrative around each turn. There is nothing like the view as you approach the first turn – scary normally, but comforting to know the bus is only going 35 mph! The start/finish line has one strip of the original brick track. The black and white checkered victory circle actually raises the winning car and driver high into the air so all spectators can see. You'll also get a view of Gasoline Alley where drivers and mechanics spend pre-race time pampering their cars. The gift shop has no trouble selling souvenirs to the starry-eyed visitors who can only dream of such speed.

INDIANAPOLIS ZOO/ WHITE RIVER GARDENS

1200 West Washington Street (in White River Park from West Street exits off major interstates)

Indianapolis 46222

❑ Phone: (317) 630-2001

   Web: www.indyzoo.com and www.whiterivergardens.com

❑ Hours: Daily 9:00am - 4:00pm. (Extended Hours, April-July). Closed Monday and Tuesday (January-February). Gardens have more restricted hours, especially Fall and Winter seasons.

❑ Admission: GARDENS: $6.50 adult, $5.50 senior, $4.50 child (3-12). ZOO: $10.75 adult, $7.75 senior, $6.75 child (3-12). Reduced prices in winter months.

❑ Miscellaneous: Stroller rental. Parking $3.00. Gift shop.

The 64 acre cageless zoo is home to simulated habitats featuring deserts, plains, forests and the ocean. Get inspired in the Gardens by the most unique and beautiful botanical attraction in the Midwest. Highlights are the Water Garden, Sun & Shade Gardens, and, for kids especially, the Motion Garden and the Mist Garden. Here's some things to look for:

❑ <u>WATERS BIOME</u> - consists of the Dolphin Pavilion, the Waters Building housing the Zoo's fish, marine birds, amphibians and the Amazon exhibit, and the walrus, seal, sea lion and polar bear marine mammal exhibits. The only dolphin shows in Indiana are daily (at performance or underwater level).

❑ <u>DESERTS BIOME</u> - The 80-foot diameter transparent dome allows the animals to bask in natural sunlight year-round while heating and air conditioning vents hidden in the rocks keep the temperature in the 80's. Free roaming desert plants and animals co-exist as they would in nature. Giant cacti, lizards, and iguanas roam the dome.

❑ <u>ENCOUNTERS AREA</u> - domestic animal shows and interaction with zookeepers and animals. "EdZootainment" combines education and entertainment.

❏ FORESTS BIOME - include Amur (Siberian) tigers, golden lion tamarins, and red pandas. Lena, one of the Zoo's Amur tigers, was wild-caught in Siberia after poachers shot her mother.

❏ PLAINS BIOME - kudu and zebras grazing in their large yard along with ostriches, vultures and other birds, giraffes pluck leaves from trees, and elephants. East African crowned cranes and Marabou storks rest near a pond or see African lions, African elephants and African wild dogs.

Also, check out the train rides, antique carousel, horse-drawn trolley or pony, camel and elephant rides. The adventuresome will like the only Indy coaster, Kombo safari family coaster.

INDIANAPOLIS INDIANS BASEBALL

501 West Maryland Street (games at Victory Field)

Indianapolis 46225

❏ Phone: (317) 269-3542, **Web: www.minorleaguebaseball.com**

The AAA American Association Indians play games at Victory Field, April to early September. The Indians are affiliated with the Milwaukee Brewers and have been Indianapolis' professional baseball team since 1887.

INDIANAPOLIS RACEWAY PARK

10267 E. US Hwy 136

Indianapolis 46234

❏ Phone: (317) 293-RACE or (800) 884-6472 tickets
Web: www.irponline.com
❏ Season: March - October.

IRP features three unique tracks, drawing the biggest names in racing from the NHRA to NASCAR and USAC for annual events at the complex (US National Drag Racing, midgets, sprints, USAC Silver Crown and Kroger Speedfest).

INDIANA BLAST AND BLAZE AND VORTEX SOCCER

PO Box 50980, **Indianapolis** 46250

❑   Phone: (317) 585-9203

The Blast (men's professional A-League team) and Blaze (women's W-League team) play from May to September at Kuntz Stadium on West 16th Street. Family tickets are available. The Indiana Vortex, the state's only professional indoor team, plays in the fall and winter in the World Indoor Soccer League.

INDIANAPOLIS COLTS

7001 West 56th Street (home games in the RCA Dome)

Indianapolis 46254

❑   Phone: (317) 297-7000, **Web: www.colts.com**

NFL Football and the Colts Kids Club package are a little football fan's dream.

MORGAN-MONROE STATE FOREST

6220 Forest Road (8 miles east of SR 37)

Martinsville 46151

❑   Phone: (765) 342-4026
       Web: www.state.in.us/dnr/forestry/property/morgmonr.htm
❑   Miscellaneous: Camping, Hiking trails.

Morgan-Monroe State Forest encompasses more than 24,000 acres in Morgan and Monroe counties in south central Indiana. The forest land encompasses many steep ridges and valleys, and is forested with some of the state's finest hardwoods. The original settlers of the area cleared and attempted to farm the ridges, but were frustrated by rocky soil unsuitable for agriculture. The highlight here might be Draper Cabin (if you can get a reservation). The use of this cabin is a unique experience. No other

Indiana state forest offers the opportunity to rent an old log cabin and return to a time 110 years ago when the fireplace provided heat and food was prepared over the burning coals. Three forest lakes, Bryant Creek Lake (9 acres), Cherry Lake (4 acres) and Prather Lake (4 acres) are all open to fishing and boating, but not swimming. Gold Panning is permitted in Morgan-Monroe and Yellowwood State Forests.

ALEXANDER CARRIAGE RIDES

Franklin and VanBuren Streets (Next to Old Bartley House)

Nashville 47448

- ❏ Phone: (812) 988-8230
- ❏ Hours: Daily, weather permitting
- ❏ Tours: Horse-drawn carriage rides with Tim, the driver and his horse, Dan.
- ❏ Miscellaneous: Interesting sites are pointed out throughout downtown.

BROWN COUNTY HISTORICAL MUSEUM

Museum Lane, Downtown

Nashville 47448

- ❏ Phone: (812) 988-6089
- ❏ Hours: Weekends and Holidays 1:00-5 :00pm. (May-October)
- ❏ Admission: Donations
- ❏ Miscellaneous: 1897 Doctor's Office, blacksmith, loom room, 1879 log jail (men were kept downstairs, women upstairs) and 1850's pioneer cabin.

BROWN COUNTY STATE PARK
State Road 46 East or West
Nashville 47448

❑   Phone: (812) 988-6406
   Web: www.in.gov/dnr/parklake/parks/brownco.html
❑   Admission: $3.00-$5.00 per vehicle.

Cabins & Abe Martin Lodge. (812) 988-4418. Accommodations and Restaurant. Nearby excursions are at Yellowwood State Forest (rare trees) or T.C. Steele State Memorial. Indiana's largest state park also has camping, horse camping and riding trails, hiking trails, naturalist services, scenic driving, picnicking, fishing and swimming.

MELCHIOR MARIONETTE THEATRE
South VanBuren Street (west side of street)
Nashville 47448

❑   Phone: (800) 849-4853
   www.nashville-indiana.com/Attractions/puppet/show.html
❑   Shows: 1:00 & 3:00 pm, Saturday & Sunday (July-October)
❑   Admission: $2.50 general (popcorn is free), purchased 15
   minutes before Showtime at the theatre. Call for schedule.

Second and third generations of Melchiors specialize in performing with beautiful hand-crafted and costumed marionettes. The charming sixty seat outdoor theatre in downtown Nashville is where the half-life size handcrafted marionettes perform 20 minute Cabaret shows.

NASHVILLE EXPRESS TRAIN TOURS
Franklin and Van Buren Streets
Nashville 47448

❏   Phone: (812) 988-2355 or (812) 988-2308
❏   Hours: Daily 10:00am-8:00pm (April-October)
❏   Admission: $4.00 (ages 5+)
❏   Tours: 2.5 mile narrated tour of downtown. Pickup at major motels every 30 minutes.

Simulated steam locomotive train offers a 2.5-mile narrated tour of downtown Nashville.

T.C. STEELE STATE HISTORIC SITE
4220 South T.C Steele Road (1.5 miles south of Hwy 46 at Belmont, off SR 4)
Nashville 47448

❏   Phone: (812) 988-2785
❏   Hours: Tuesday-Saturday 9:00am-5:00pm, Sunday 1:00-5:00pm (mid December-mid March). Closed Thanksgiving, Christmastime, New Years and Easter.
❏   Admission: FREE, donations accepted.

The site is Theodore Clement Steele's (1847-1926), a noted Indiana artist's, home and studio. See exhibits of Impressionistic paintings by the Hoosier Group painter. Surrounding nature preserves provide inspiration. Guided tours are offered through "The House of the Singing Winds" and the Large Studio where changing exhibits display paintings done throughout Steele's life. The 211-acre site includes four hiking trails, the Dewar Log Cabin and the 92-acre Selma Steele Nature Preserve.

YELLOWWOOD STATE FOREST

772 South Yellowwood Road

Nashville 47448

❑   Phone: (812) 988-7945
     Web: www.in.gov/dnr/forestry/property/ylwwd.htm

Yellowwood offers 23,400 wooded acres with three primitive lakes, camping, biking, horse and hiking trails, nature study, fishing, and boat rental. Panning for gold is permitted on Morgan-Monroe and Yellowwood State Forests. A gold panning permit is required. The permit, which can be obtained free of charge, allows for panning gold on a hobby basis. Yellowwood State Forest is named for a tree common in the mid-south but rare this far north. The yellowwood tree (Cladrastis kentukea) has bright yellow heartwood that is hard and dense. The tree flowers abundantly but only every three to five years in the spring with loose clusters of pea-like, fragrant white flowers. Less than 200 acres in Yellowwood support the yellowwood tree on north facing slopes and deep ravines near Crooked Creek Lake.

CANTERBURY ARABIANS

12131 East 196th Street

Noblesville 46060

❑   Phone: (317) 776-0779,
❑   Hours: Daily 8:00am-5:00pm (call first)
❑   Admission: FREE
❑   Tours: By appointment

Visit with "Real Mac" – a former Indianapolis Colt's Mascot. Lovers of Arabians get to visit a real working horse farm. See bathing, eating, or a foal being born. Best visiting time is Spring/Summer when new colts arrive.

HAMILTON COUNTY MUSEUM OF HISTORY

Noblesville Square, PO Box 397

Noblesville 46060

- ❑ Phone: (317) 770-0775
- ❑ Hours: Thursday-Saturday 10:00am-4:00pm, Sunday 1:00-4:00pm (Summer).
- ❑ Admission: FREE, donations accepted.

An 1875 museum that is the old Sheriff's residence and Jail features more than 100 items.

HAMILTON COUNTY THEATRE/ BELFRY THEATRE

SR 238

Noblesville 46060

- ❑ Phone: (317) 773-0398, **Web: www.hctb.org**
- ❑ Season: (September-July) Call for reservations and show schedule.
- ❑ Admission: $8.00-$10.00

Enjoy theatrical productions like "Charlottes Web" and "The Secret Garden." One of Indiana's oldest and most honored community theaters, the company produces six family-oriented comedies, dramas, and musicals annually.

INDIANA TRANSPORTATION MUSEUM

325 Cicero Road (Forest Park and SR19)

Noblesville 46060

- ❑ Phone: (317) 773-6000, **Web: www.itm.org**
- ❑ Hours: Tuesday-Sunday 10:00am-5:00pm (Memorial Day-Labor Day). Weekends only (April, May, September, October).
- ❑ Admission: $3.00 adult, $2.00 child (3-12)

Indiana Transportation Museum (cont.)

❑   Miscellaneous: Train rides additional charge.

Ride to the Indiana State Fair or just a simple tour on an authentic steam or diesel train. Tour 50 rail cars with antics and stories from retired railroad volunteers. Artifacts displayed within train cars. The private rolling hotel suite of millionaire Henry Flagler can be toured on special holidays. Trolley rides are available daily during the season, and train rides are available on weekends only.

GIANT EARTH HOME

2928 West Larry Street (Meet at Faulk Park for tours)

Pendleton 46064

❑   Phone: (765) 778-2757, **Web: www.giantearthship.com**
❑   Hours: Reservations only (May to mid-October)
❑   Admission: Adults $6.00, Students $4.00
❑   Tours: Ages 5+, tours begin with 1/2 mile nature hike.

A do-it-yourself home in the woods built by local, Vic Cook. It's powered by solar energy and full of environmental science equipment. The home is made with available materials of stone and scavenged wood. The kids' most intriguing part is the refrigerator built out of a hollowed birch log using high tech science to keep it cool.

GROVER MUSEUM / SHELBY COUNTY MUSEUM

52 W. Broadway

Shelbyville 46176

❑   Phone: (317) 392-4634
❑   Hours: Open year round, call for seasonal hours & special events.
❑   Admission: FREE, donations accepted.

Three changing galleries including a permanent Model Railroad Layout and a Street Scene with 28 buildings in 1900-1910 decor with Shelby County artifacts.

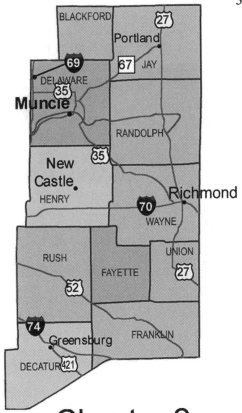

Chapter 2

Central East Area

38

Our Favorites...

National Model Aviation Museum

Muncie Children's Museum

Abbott's Candy Shop

Indiana Basketball Hall of Fame

Michael Bonne Coppersmith

Whitewater Canal Historic Site

Try your hand at coppersmithing
MICHAEL BONNE

BROOKVILLE LAKE STATE RESERVOIR

US 27 to SR 101 South

Brookville 47012

❑   Phone: (765) 647-2657
    Web: www.in.gov/dnr/parklake/reservoirs/brookville.html
❑   Admission: $3.00-$5.00
❑   Miscellaneous: Whitewater Memorial State Park nearby has
    emptied their water basin but still has "land lover" activities such
    as bridle trails and picnicking.

The Lake is situated in the picturesque Whitewater River Valley.
Whitewater rafting is king here, April-October. Recreational
activities include: Archery Range, Boating / 9 Launch Ramps,
Camping, Cultural Arts Programs, Fishing / Ice Fishing, Hiking
Trails, Horseshoe pits, Interpretive / Recreational Programs,
Marina, Swimming / 2 Beaches, and Volleyball.

BEARCREEK FARMS

8341 North 400 East (Off US 27)

Bryant 47326

❑   Phone: (260) 997-6822 or (800) 288-7630
    Web: www.bearcreekfarms.com
❑   Showtimes for Theatre: Tuesday-Saturday 2:00pm & 7:30pm,
    Sunday at 2:00pm. (April-December). Resort open daily from
    March to December. Some shops and museum open Mid-April
    thru October.
❑   Admission: Resort grounds - FREE. Shows are $10.00 adult,
    $5.00 child. Family Day Sunday all shows are $8.00 per person.
    Lodging is moderately priced.
❑   Miscellaneous: Christmas themed shows run November till
    Christmastime. Additional Saturday Show at 9:15pm.

If you're in town or spending the night at one of their country
cabins on the property, you'll have a variety of activities to choose
from depending on the season (check their website for seasonal

packages). The Ole Swimming Hole indoor pool has twisty waterslides for all ages and Indoor mini-golf (sm. Fee). The Goodtime Theatre features live high energy musical performances filled with theatrical themes like country, the 50's or Patriotism. The Tin Lizzy Museum is a place where you can enjoy a tribute to Henry Ford and his contribution to the industrial revolution. While visiting Bearcreek Farms Country Resort do not forget to visit the Homestead Restaurant (open daily for lunch and dinner) and numerous gift shops.

HUDDLESTON FARMHOUSE MUSEUM

838 National Road (US 40 West)

Cambridge City 47327

- ❑   Phone: (765) 478-3172
- ❑   Hours: Tuesday-Saturday 10:00am-4:00pm (Year round - except January). Sunday 1:00-4:00pm. (May-August Only)
- ❑   Admission: Suggested donation $3.00 per person.
- ❑   Tours: Guided tours by appointment.
- ❑   Miscellaneous: Theme days like Dairy Days and Harvest Supper plus many historical re-enactments.

Experience the life of an early pioneer farming family who opened their home to travelers for meals, provisions, shelter and feed/rest for horses. John and Susannah's home was built between 1839 and 1841 and includes a restored barn, three-story farmhouse, a springhouse and smokehouse. Many of the family's personal possessions like wooden bowls and special occasion parlor chairs, plus essentials for eleven children are displayed. Our favorite part of the tour was the basement where the Huddleston's apparently rented two "travelers' kitchens" used for cooking and sleeping.

WHITEWATER VALLEY RAILROAD

300 S Eastern Avenue (Downtown)

Connersville 47331

❑   Phone: (765) 825-2054, **Web: www.whitewatervalleyrr.org**
❑   Hours: Saturdays, Sundays, Holidays at Noon (May-October) EST.
❑   Admission: $14.00 adult, $7.00 child (2-12)
❑   Tours: Start at Noon. 2 hour stop, returns at 6:00pm. Early train (10:00 am) in October (Thursday & Friday).
❑   Miscellaneous: Bring a sack lunch to eat while on the train. Sit-down meals in stop at Metamora. Gift Shop with extensive "Thomas The Train" items.

Indiana's Longest Scenic Railroad provides a 32 mile round trip on a historic locomotive #25. There are vintage Stillwell open window coaches and a restored woodside caboose that ride along the Whitewater River past dams, gristmills and the canal tow path.

LEVI COFFIN HOUSE STATE HISTORIC HOUSE

113 US 27 (6 miles North of I-70 - Exit 151)

Fountain City 47341

❑   Phone: (765) 847-2432
    Web: www.waynet.org/nonprofit/coffin.htm
❑   Hours: Tuesday-Saturday 1:00-4:00pm (June-August). Saturday only, 1:00-4:00pm (September-October)
❑   Admission: $2.00 adult, $1.00 child (6-18)
❑   Tours: Pre-scheduled school groups $0.50/person

Owned by the Coffins, this was an eight room refuge and rest home for slaves (up to 2000 total) on their escape North. The stop was part of the Underground Railroad so named because it was a secret stop between destinations. Some would stay a few days and others weeks until they felt well enough to travel on. You'll get to see the second floor hiding place. The owners, Levi and Catharine are characterized as Simeon and Rachael Halliday in the story "Uncle Tom's Cabin". This stop was so successful that all of the slaves who stopped here eventually reached freedom. What does the number of roses in a vase in the front window symbolize?

ABBOTT'S CANDY SHOP

48 East Walnut (I-70 to SR 1 to SR 38 [Left] to Perry [Left] to Walnut [Right])

Hagerstown 47346

❑   Phone: (765) 489-4442, **Web: www.abbottscandy.com**
❑   Hours: Candy Shop: Monday-Friday 9:00am-5:00pm. Also open Saturdays 9:00am-5:00pm during Winter Holiday Season. Observation area within shop is open when store is open. No reserved tour required for caramel observation kitchen.
❑   Admission: FREE
❑   Tours: Except Thanksgiving - Christmas. By appointment. 3rd grade+. Best before 11:30am, not Lunch time.
❑   Miscellaneous: 1st visit entitles you to one free sample of caramel wrapped right off the line.

Founded in the 1890's and still owned by the Abbott family members, they are nationally famous for their homemade caramels and chocolates made from 100 year old recipes. See the caramels made from scratch. First, butter is boiled in copper kettles and then milk and sugar are added. It was fun to hear the cook yell "CARAMEL!" just at the time it's finished cooking. The other ladies hurry over to help pour out the hot mixture on cold marble slabs. After it cools, the caramels are cut using a hand crank and each morsel is wrapped individually in white wax paper or sent over to the chocolate room. After leaving the kitchen, the tour moves into the "chocolate room" where the various centers are coated with chocolate. Cream centers are formed by hand or by using dies and a hand press. Caramels that are to be covered in chocolate are specially cut to size and the various nut and caramel clusters are made in the kitchen using a large depositor to drop hot caramel onto beds of nutmeats. You'll love their line of funny-named candies called Gismo, Gisnut, Gishew and Gismond. Can you guess which nut belongs in each candy?

CARTHAGE, KNIGHTSTOWN AND SHIRLEY RAILROAD TRAIN

112 West Carey Street (I-70 to SR 109 Exit South Downtown)

Knightstown 46148

- ❑ Phone: (765) 345-5561 or (800) 345-2704
  Web: http://cksrailroad.homestead.com/TrainRides.html
- ❑ Hours: Friday-Sunday & Holidays 10:30am-4:30pm (May-October).
- ❑ Admission: $7.00 adult, $5.00 child (3-11).
- ❑ Tours: 1 hour, 15 minutes round trip. Departure at 11:00 am, 1:00 & 3:00 pm on Saturday & Sunday & Holidays. Only departure 11:00am on Fridays.
- ❑ Miscellaneous: Quick stop in Carthage for a snack. Group rates 20+. Train Robbery trips in May, June and August. Gift Shop.

Sit in the coach or caboose as it heads south passing under a railroad bridge and through the countryside ranging from cornfields to woodland ravines, past the Big Blue River or a working sawmill. The covered platform car (once part of a New York Central passenger and freight station) serves as a spot to ride those in strollers or wheelchairs. As the engine is "run around" for the return trip, you can view rail equipment displays as you get off to stretch you legs.

MICHAEL BONNE COPPERSMITH

224 East Main Street (I-70 to SR 109 to US 40E)

Knightstown 46148

- ❑ Phone: (765) 345-5521, **Web: www.michaelbonne.com**
- ❑ Hours: Monday-Saturday 9:00am-5:00pm
- ❑ Admission: FREE

Michael Bonne Coppersmith (cont.)

❑   Tours: By appointment. School age. Monday-Friday only.
❑   Miscellaneous: Showroom with copper treasures housed in a tin ceiling and pine floored old department store. Cookie cutters, trays, bowls, ornaments, etc.

After Michael had a serious disabling head injury in the early 1980's, he needed a craft to occupy his time. His authentic, trendy, and replica copper crafts caught lots of attention. They are so well known now, even Martha Stewart has a designer line that Mr. Bonne's shop creates. On tour you will start at the beginning seeing large sheets of copper cut, then curled or flattened, shaped using all manual antique tools, and finally soldered (attaching ends) and scrubbed. The museum-style workshop is adapted from a 19th century sheet metal shop. A "Santa's Workshop" atmosphere – choose the "Hammer your own, hands on workshop" – for $1.00/person a coppersmith helps you create your own ornament. First choose from objects like ducks, angels, gingerbread men or stars. Next you're given a weathered hammer with one flat and one rounded end. Now, begin hammering your piece of copper over a wood block to your heart's delight! When you've achieved that "old colonial look" you can stop and hole punch the top. You now have a personalized souvenir for the tree – and the best souvenir of all – hand made.

WHITEWATER CANAL STATE HISTORIC SITE

19083 Clayborn Street (8 miles West of Brookville, US 52)

Metamora 47030

❑   Phone: (765) 647-6512, **Web: www.ai.org/ism/sites/whitewater**
❑   Hours: Tuesday-Saturday 9:00am-5:00pm, Sunday 1:00-5:00pm. (mid-March to mid-December). Closed Thanksgiving, Christmastime, New Years and Easter.
❑   Admission: Free

❏ Tours: 30 Minute Canal boat tour, $1.00 /person. Tuesday-Sunday 1:00-4:00pm (May-October).

❏ Miscellaneous: Gristmill on site grinds grain for purchase.

Originally a town built around the canal between 1836-1847. The canal rides go through an 80 ft. covered wooden aqueduct lifting the canal waters 16 ft. above the creek. Also pass by a restored lock and by a gristmill. Hundreds of cute little shops (they made the stores very small, scaled down, mini-village look). This is a full day excursion - if you don't mind crowds, we especially love all the extra activity and entertainment during festival weekends.

WILBUR WRIGHT BIRTHPLACE AND MUSEUM

Wilbur Wright Road, 1525 N CR 750E (just South of US 36 & North of SR 38; I-70 exit 131, follow signs)

Millville 47346

❏ Phone: (765) 332-2495
Web: www.geocities.com/Heartland/Forest/8737/

❏ Hours: Monday-Saturday 10:00am-5:00pm, Sunday 1:00-5:00pm (April-October)

❏ Admission: $2.50 adult, $1.50 child, $7.00 family rate.

❏ Miscellaneous: Gift Shop. Shelter/picnic area. RC air strip

Wilbur and brother, Orville (born later in Dayton) turned the dream of flight into reality. A life-size replica of the Wright Flyer and sample of a wind tunnel are on display next to the birthplace home of the Wright family filled with memorabilia like shoes and toys. This is where Wilbur took his first step as a baby. Learn about intimate facets of their family and faith.

NATIONAL MODEL AVIATION MUSEUM / ACADEMY OF MODEL AERONAUTICS

5151 East Memorial Drive (SR 67 East by-pass to Memorial exit)

Memorial Exit), **Muncie** 47302

- ❑ Phone: (765) 287-1256 or (800) 435-9262
  Web: www.modelaircraft.org/site/museum.htm
- ❑ Hours: Monday-Friday 8:00am-4:30pm, Saturday-Sunday
  10:00am-4:00pm. EST. Closed Sundays from Thanksgiving thru
  Easter. Special holiday hours.
- ❑ Admission: $2.00 adult, $1.00 child (6-17). Flying site admission
  is free.
- ❑ Miscellaneous: Gift Shop with souvenirs plus educational books
  and kits. National Championships in July and August.

Colorful model planes hang above you as you wander through many well-designed displays that comprise the largest collection of memorabilia and flying models in the world. The types of flying miniature craft include free-flight, indoor, control line (lines connect the model and pilot), radio control and scale models. Look close for the plaques identifying world-record holders. The 1000 acre exhibit and competition fields showcase the only form of aviation open to everyone. We were there for a rocket launch event.... 3 - 2 - 1 … LIFT OFF! A few moments after lift off, the rocket's parachute floats back to earth. The friendly participants evoke interest in the sport.

MINNETRISTA CULTURE CENTER AND OAKHURST GARDENS

1200 North Minnetrista Parkway (just north of Downtown)

Muncie 47303

- ❑ Phone: (765) 282-4848 or (800) 4CULTURE
  Web: www.mccoak.org
- ❑ Hours: Monday-Friday 9:00am-5:30pm, Saturday 9:00am-
  8:00pm, Sunday 11:00am-5:30pm.

❑   Admission: $5.00 adult, $3.00 senior, $3.00 student (under 12),
     $15.00 family.
❑   Miscellaneous: Gift shop with educational toys and art. Free
     Summer outdoor concerts. Saturday Kids Club.

"Minnetrista" means "a gathering place by the water". A series of impressive large columns greet you at the entrance. They are all that remains of the F.C. Ball house destroyed by fire in 1967. Favorite exhibits usually revolve around lasers, virtual reality, or hologram displays. Explore exhibits on Indiana's art and history such as The State of the Game: Why Indiana Became Basketball Country. Experience first-hand world class traveling science exhibits like Antarctica and Dinosaurs. Oakhurst Gardens is the home and gardens of elegant Victorian heiress to Ball Corporation canning jars. The Discovery Cabin for the kids is where they can explore nature hands-on.

MUNCIE CHILDREN'S MUSEUM

515 South High Street (off I-69 exit 41 to SR 332, follow signs, adj.
To Convention Center)

Muncie 47305

❑   Phone: (765) 286-1660, **www.munciechildrensmuseum.com**
❑   Hours: Tuesday-Saturday 10:00am-5:00pm, Sunday 1:00-
     5:00pm.
❑   Admission: $5.00 general (ages 1-100 years)
❑   Miscellaneous: Gift Shop. Annual membership available

This hands-on museum is designed to stimulate curiosity and imagination. Older kids may want to head straight upstairs where they can hold small animals and snakes or to the Outdoor Learning Center. Experience Indiana from several points of view - a forest treehouse, a farm and pond or a limestone quarry. Younger ones will gravitate to the dress-up clothes and take the challenge of climbing through giant landscapes. Next, they might build a sand castle, play with waterways or pretend to be a storekeeper in a simulated town. Leave enough time for the best display - Garfield. This is the only permanent Garfield display in the world (could be here because creator Jim Davis lives in Muncie). The highlight of our trip had to be co-starring in a short Garfield cartoon. For a small fee, you can record this family treasure of members of your family zapped into a Garfield skit and actually interacting with him. As you watch in a monitor, Garfield casually instructs you to jump, dance, stop or run with him. It's a blast!

HENRY COUNTY HISTORICAL MUSEUM

606 South 14th Street

New Castle 47362

- ❑ Phone: (765) 529-4028
  Web: www.kiva.net/~hchisoc/museum.htm
- ❑ Hours: Monday-Saturday 1:00-4:30pm
- ❑ Admission: $2.00 adult, $1.00 student, FREE children.

This former house owned by General William Grose, a commander during the Civil War is the setting for examples of artifacts from local history. Clothing, musical instruments, tools, a barbershop and authentically decorated and furnished rooms as the Grose family would have lived.

INDIANA BASKETBALL HALL OF FAME MUSEUM

One Hall of Fame Court (I-70 to SR 3 North Exit, 5 miles)

New Castle 47362

- ❑ Phone: (765) 529-1891, **Web: www.hoopshall.com**
- ❑ Hours: Tuesday-Saturday 10:00am-5:00pm, Sunday 1:00-5:00 pm. Closed Thanksgiving, Christmas Eve, Christmas, New Year's Eve, New Year's Day, and Easter.
- ❑ Admission: $4.00 adult, $2.00 child (5-12)
- ❑ Tours: 20+ people, reduced rates.

❏   Miscellaneous: Gift Shop. Favorite (and most crowded) time to
       visit is early Spring for the start of the basketball season called
       "March Madness".

The Indiana Basketball Hall of Fame Museum captures the essence
of "Hoosier Hysteria" and helps explain to the visitor why the
game of basketball has a special place in the hearts and minds of
folks from this state.   The Hall focuses on Indiana high school
players and coaches, men and women. On display are signed balls,
jerseys and trophies. Visit the MARSH THEATER, where visitors
can experience the emotion of the state tournament.   Step inside
the locker room to hear one of COACH JOHN WOODEN'S
inspirational pep talks. Test your knowledge of basketball trivia on
a computer game or pretend you're playing for the winning shot in
the final seconds of a game!

SUMMIT LAKE STATE PARK

5993 North Messick Road (Off US 36)

New Castle 47362

❏   Phone: (765) 766-5873
       Web: www.in.gov/dnr/parklake/parks/summitlake.html
❏   Admission: $3.00-$5.00 per vehicle.

An expansive view and good fishing will beckon you to this park
with more than 2,550 acres including a large lake. Facilities
include 125 Class "A" campsites, 3 boat ramps, a beach bathhouse
and 2 large open shelters which can be reserved for family picnics
and other events. Summit Lake has an excellent bird watching and
wildlife observation area and fishing, boating & rentals and hiking
trails.

ME'S ZOO

CR 500 South, 12441 West Randolph (Follow sign 4 miles East on
SR 32 to CR 700 East to CR 500)

Parker City 47368

❑   Phone: (765) 468-8559
❑   Hours: Tuesday-Thursday, Saturday 10:00am-6:00pm (late April-
     September)
❑   Admission: Approximately $5.00 per person.

This privately owned zoo has over 32 acres include a petting area
and picnic/concession area. Small, fenced-in sections give you a
clear view of all the animals. Because it's a "petite zoo", children
(ages 2 - 8 years) enjoy it most (not overwhelming). Look for
bears, camels, zebras, monkeys, tigers, and exotic talking birds.

HAYES REGIONAL ARBORETUM

801 Elks Road (I-70 Exit 156A west on U.S. 40 approx. 2 miles)

Richmond 47374

❑   Phone: (765) 962-3745, **Web: www.hayesarboretum.org**
❑   Hours: Tuesday-Saturday 9:00am-5:00pm, Sunday 1:00- 5:00pm.
     Closed Sundays Christmas thru Easter.
❑   Admission: FREE. $3.00/vehicle for auto tour.

The 355 acre nature preserve with 179 woody plants native to the
region, has the 1st solar greenhouse. There are five hiking trails
and snowshoeing in the winter (snowshoes provided). The Old
1833 Dairy Barn Nature Center has exhibits, a gift shop and a bird
sanctuary.

JOSEPH MOORE MUSEUM OF NATURAL HISTORY

Earlham College Campus - US 40 West

Richmond 47374

❑   Phone: (765) 983-1303
     Web: www.waynet.wayne.in.us/nonprofit/jos_moore.htm

❑   Hours: Monday, Wednesday, Friday 1:00-4:00pm. (September-
      April). Sunday 1:00 - 5:00pm (all year)
❑   Admission: FREE
❑   Tours: Staffed by students by appointment.

Found here are an Egyptian mummy and pre-historic animals like a
mastodon, allosaurus skeletons and fossils. Mammals and birds are
displayed in natural habitats typical of Indiana. Hold a LIVE
snake! Some highlights include: The Ralph Teetor Planetarium,
Indiana Birds of Prey Exhibit, Invertebrate Fossils and Geology
Exhibit - displays geological specimens from the local limestone,
African Mammal Display, Arthropod Exhibit, Mammal Alcove -
displays Indiana mammals in their natural habitat, Marsh Birds
Display, Paleontology area - includes skeletons of a mastodon, a
giant beaver, a dire wolf, a giant ground sloth, and an allosaurus,
and the Discovery Room - with hands-on exhibits that encourage
children and adults to touch.

RICHMOND ROOSTERS PROFESSIONAL BASEBALL

201 NW 13th Street (games played at Don McBride Stadium)

Richmond 47374

❑   Phone: (765) 935-PLAY, **Web: www.richmondroosters.com**
❑   Hours: Season runs June - August
❑   Admission: $4.00 general, $1.00 off any ticket for children and
      seniors (age 5+).

Class "A" independent Frontier League. Ice Cream Sundays,
Family Fun Nights and Rooster Cookouts are some of their family-
friendly promotions. Look for the Rowdy Rooster mascot.

WAYNE COUNTY HISTORICAL MUSEUM

1150 North "A" Street, downtown

Richmond 47374

- ❑　Phone: (765) 962-5756, **Web: www.wchm.org**
- ❑　Hours: Tuesday-Friday 9:00am-4:00pm, Saturday - Sunday 1:00-4:00pm.
- ❑　Admission: $4.00 adult, $2.00 child (5-17).

Collections of Egyptian mummies (laid flat in a clear chest with push-button lighting for an X-ray effect), 1929 Davis airplane, Richmond-made cars and a Woolen desk. There is also a General Store indoors and an Outdoor Pioneer Village (site of many pioneer festivals).

WHITEWATER GORGE PARK

64 Waterfall Road at Brookville Lake (2200 US 40 East)

Richmond 47374

- ❑　Phone: (765) 983-7275, **Web: www.hayesarboretum.org**
- ❑　Hours: Daily, Dawn to Dusk
- ❑　Admission: FREE

Fossil collecting with geologic information available to play pretend archaeologists. The Gorge formed during the Ice Age and has many vertical cliffs surrounding Thistlethwaite Falls. The fossils you will find here are from skeletons of animals that lived years ago on the bottom of a warm shallow sea that covered this area. Some of the fossils you may find are clams, snails, corals, trilobites, and many more. Thistlethwaite Falls is a fun place to wade in the water. Walking tours and geological information are available at the Richmond Parks & Recreation Office.

WINCHESTER SPEEDWAY

2556 W SR 32 (I-70 Exit 151 US 27 north (from Richmond)
approximately 22 miles to SR 32 west 2 1/2 miles)

Winchester 47394

❑   Phone: (765) 584-9701, **Web: www.winchesterspeedway.com**

USAC sprints, midget and stock cars (NASCAR) on world's fastest ½ mile banked track.

Chapter 3
Central West Area

Our Favorites...

Billie Creek Village

Wolf Park

Tippecanoe Battlefield

Historical Museum
of Wabash Valley

Bison / Wolf Challenge at Wolf Park

TIPPECANOE BATTLEFIELD

(SR 43 off I-65 Follow signs)

Battle Ground 47920

❑   Phone: (765) 567-2147
     Web: www.tcha.mus.in.us/battlefield.htm
❑   Hours: Daily 10:00am-5:00pm (March-November). Daily
     10:00am-4:00pm (December-February). Closed Thanksgiving,
     Christmas, and New Years.
❑   Admission: $3.00 adult, $2.00 senior, $1.00 child (age 5+)
❑   Miscellaneous: Interpretive Center museum and gift shop.
     Afternoon Adventure 3rd Saturday of each month - create 1800's
     crafts, 2:00-4:00 pm. Approximately $20.00 per family. Also,
     monthly camp-ins, grades 4-6. Picnic/Shelter Grounds. Nature
     Center open April-October.

A significant spot where (because of the lack of unity between
Tecumseh and The Prophet), the American Indian lost his final
grip on the Midwest land he had roamed for thousands of years.
Also, the same spot served for a rally in May, 1840 when over
30,000 people followed poor roads and trails to sing the praises of
"Old Tipp" - General William Henry Harrison who had 28 years
earlier bloodily claimed this battle ground for the Territory. The
modern, festive political campaigns of today may have originated
from the rally where roast beef, pork, stew and bread were served
free. Catchy campaign songs capitalized the great presidency
slogan, "Tippecanoe and Tyler, too!" as bands, speeches, floats
and tales of the battle added flavor to the event. The museum has a
fiber optic map detailing moves of soldiers and Indians. Two slide
shows in theaters explain the progress of events that led to
conflicts fought here. The Battlefield has markers where officers
died in battles. Your family leaves this site with a deep
appreciation of the causes (right or wrong) of hatred and fame of
the men who held their ideals so closely.

WOLF PARK

4012 East 800 North (I-65 exit 178, SR 43 north to SR 225 east to downtown, follow signs)

Battle Ground 47920

- ❑ Phone: (765) 567-2265, **Web: www.wolfpark.org**
- ❑ Hours: Tuesday-Sunday 1:00-5:00pm. Best time is weekends. (May-November)
- ❑ Admission: $4.00 - $5.00 adult, $3.00 child (6-13)
- ❑ Tours: Recommended. Reservations recommended.
- ❑ Miscellaneous: Special Wolf-Bison presentations on Sundays at 1:00 pm where they challenge each other's herd. Wolf Howl Nights on Saturdays at 7:30 pm year-round (also Fridays nights from May-November)... listen to howling, communicating chorus and try to imitate. Weather permitting.

You'll see the herd of bison first as you enter (their faces are so-o-o large!) and then in another caged area, the foxes (the red fox looks just like Todd from "The Fox and The Hound"). A quarter mile walk takes you and your guide to see the packs of gray wolves in an actual social structure. See them eat (prepared "recycled" animal road kill), quarrel and rest - at a fairly close distance. Learn why the lower class of wolves always get picked on. You won't leave without an authentic chorus of howls from the pack. Even in broad daylight, those calls are very eerie! The coyote is always the loudest - showy! Be sure to try to come on weekends when the special programs (see Miscellaneous above) are featured. OW--oool.

CLAY CITY POTTERY

510 East 14th Street (Corner of SR 156 South and 14th Street)

Clay City 47841

- ❑ Phone: (800) 776-2596, **Web: www.claycitypottery.com**
- ❑ Hours: Monday-Friday 8:30am-4:30pm, Saturday 8:00am-Noon. EST

For updates visit our website: www.kidslovepublications.com

- ❑   Admission: FREE
- ❑   Tours: Pre-arranged
- ❑   Miscellaneous: Pottery Festival 2nd weekend in June.

Table-safe stoneware produced by a pottery factory. Owned by the 4th generation of the Griffith family. They are the only working commercial stoneware potters in Indiana. The hand-jiggered process of molding (pressing out water) is a very interesting manufacturing step; however, the kids seem to like the raw clay best. The large conveyor drying kilns keep things warm - we recommend tours in tempered weather.

CAGLES MILL LAKE STATE RESERVOIR

1317 West Lieber Road (Lieber State Recreation Area)

Cloverdale 46120

- ❑   Phone: (765) 795-4576
       Web: www.in.gov/dnr/parklake/reservoirs/caglesmill.html
- ❑   Admission: $3.00-$5.00 per vehicle.

Most come for the Activity Center and Water Safari Boat Tours. Other facilities include: Sport Courts, Boating, Camping, Cultural Arts Programs, Fishing (handicapped, too), Hiking, Interpretive Programs, Rentals-Boats, Pontoons, Swimming in lake or pool w/waterslide, and Water-skiing.

BEN HUR MUSEUM

(Wallace Avenue & Pike Avenue)

Crawfordsville 47933

- ❑   Phone: (765) 362-5769, **Web: www.ben-hur.com**
- ❑   Hours: Wednesday & Saturday 10:00am-4:30pm, Tuesday & Sunday 1:00-4:30pm (Summer). Tuesday - Sunday 1:00-4:30pm (April, May, September, October). Weekends only 1:00-4:30pm (March, November).
- ❑   Admission: Small (age 6+)
- ❑   Tours: By appointment year round.

Ben Hur Museum (cont.)

General Lew Wallace built this as his private library and a quiet place where he could write novels such as the famous "Ben Hur." He was also an artist, violinist and inventor. Memorabilia include Wallace's roles as a Civil War general, lawyer, state senator, scholar, and artist.

ERNIE PYLE STATE HISTORIC SITE

SR 71 Downtown, 120 Briarwood (1 mile North of US 36)

Dana 47847

- ❑ Phone: (765) 665-3633, **Web: www.in.gov/ism/sites/erniepyle/**
- ❑ Hours: Wednesday-Saturday 9:00am-5:00pm, Sunday 1:00-5:00pm. (mid-March to mid-December). Closed Thanksgiving, Christmas Eve, Christmas Day, New Year's Day and Easter.
- ❑ Admission: FREE

Summed up by a plaque saying, "At this spot, the 77th Infantry Division lost a Buddy, Ernie Pyle, 18 April, 1945". An endearing man who wrote an aviation column for the Washington Daily News and then became a roving reporter traveling the country. He wrote of ordinary people who had a simple story to tell. In 1940, Pyle went to report on the war in Europe and America's involvement. During that assignment, he was shot by a Japanese soldier.

SHAKAMAK STATE PARK

6265 W. SR 48

Jasonville 47438

- ❑ Phone: (812) 665-2158
  Web: www.in.gov/dnr/parklake/parks/shakamak.html
- ❑ Admission: $3.00-$5.00 per vehicle.

About two-thirds of the campsites are in a wooded area, offering cool shade in the summer and beautiful fall colors in autumn. Now, they have the largest and best fishing pier in the state. People of all abilities will be able to enjoy this great fishing facility. Facilities include: Boating (Electric trolling only), Saddle Barn, Cabins, Camping, Cultural Arts Programs, Fishing / Ice Fishing, Hiking Trails, Nature Center / Interpretive Services, Rental-Paddleboat/ Rowboat, Swimming / Pool / Waterslide, Tennis, and Youth Tent Areas.

TIPPECANOE COUNTY MUSEUM FOWLER HOUSE

909 South Street

Lafayette 47901

- ❑ Phone: (765) 476-8417, **Web: www.tcha.mus.in.us/fowler.htm**
- ❑ Hours: Tuesday-Sunday 1:00-5:00 pm
- ❑ Admission: $3.00 adult, $2.00 child (4-12)
- ❑ Miscellaneous: Natural history, pioneers, Native Americans, Victorian era, railroads and industry.

IMAGINATION STATION

600 North 4th Street & Cincinnati Streets (Downtown)

Lafayette 47902

- ❑ Phone: (765) 420-7780
  Web: http://users.nlci.com/imagination/
- ❑ Hours: Friday and Sunday 1:00-5:00 pm, Saturday 10:00am-5:00pm. Scheduled group visits on weekdays.
- ❑ Admission: $3.00 adult, $2.00 child (3-12)
- ❑ Miscellaneous: Educational toys gift shop.

A hands-on space, science, engineering and technology museum for kids. See and touch a 1920's fire engine, a butterfly house, a 1910 Maxwell auto or a flight simulator. Now, pretend you're a pilot or fireman. Other activities involve the Art of Science or Dr. Dino workshops with hands-on creativity focusing on various themes.

COLUMBIAN PARK AND TROPICANOE COVE

1915 Scott Street, SR 38 (downtown, corner of Main & Scott Streets, I-65 exit SR 26)

Lafayette 47905

- ❑ Phone: (765) 771-SWIM or (765) 771-2220
- ❑ Hours: Amusement Park and Cove open daily 11:00am-7:00pm (Memorial Day-Labor Day). Zoo open daily (May-October). Park grounds open from sunrise to sunset.
- ❑ Admission: Zoo - FREE. Pool and rides, $1.00 per ride average. Cove $4.00-6.00 range. Higher rates on weekends.

It's a zoo, amusement park and aquatic center. The zoo has an aviary, "touch of country" petting zoo and an animal house. In the amusement park, you'll find a merry-go-round, train ride and several adult rides. To cool off, rent a paddle boat on the pond or swim in the 77,000 square foot pool with a 160 foot curved waterslide or the kiddie water playground. From the spiraling Banana Peel tube slide to the leisurely Cattail Crick, you're sure to find plenty of cool summertime fun at the Cove.

MANSFIELD ROLLER MILL STATE HISTORIC SITE

RR 1, Box 146C (6 miles south of US 36 off SR 59)

Mansfield 47837

- ❑ Phone: (765) 344-0741, **Web: www.in.gov/ism/sites/mansfield/**
- ❑ Hours: Friday-Saturday 9:00am-5:00pm, Sunday 1:00-5:00pm.
- ❑ Admission: FREE, donations accepted.

Overlooking Big Raccoon Creek is the rustic, old Mansfield Roller Mill which is still in operation and has been grinding with water power since the 1820's. The roller process, still used in mills today, produces more flour from the same amount of wheat. Because the roller process is fully automated, the output is greatly increased while employing only three men.

For updates visit our website: www.kidslovepublications.com

TURKEY RUN STATE PARK
Rte. 1, Box 164 (US 41 to SR 47)
Marshall 47859

❑   Phone: (765) 597-2635
    Web: www.in.gov/dnr/parklake/parks/turkeyrun.html
❑   Admission: $3.00-$5.00 per vehicle.

Turkey Run Inn (765) 597-2211. Accommodations with indoor pool. Rock-walled canyons and gorges along Sugar Creek, Planetarium, Tennis & other Games. You'll marvel at the natural geologic wonders of this beautiful park as you hike along its famous trails. Visit the Colonel Richard Lieber Cabin which commemorates the contributions of the father of Indiana's state park system.

BILLIE CREEK VILLAGE
US 36 East
Rockville 47872

❑   Phone: (765) 569-3430 village/inn or (765) 569-0252 store
    Web: www.billiecreek.org
❑   Hours: Generally, 9:00 am-5:00 pm. Adjust by season and festival. Call ahead.
❑   Admission: $3.50 general (age 5+), $3.00 senior.

A re-created 20th century village with 38 authentic buildings. As you enter the grounds, you'll pass through one of three covered bridges on the property (this area is well known for its covered bridges!). Stop in and visit a farmstead, a museum, a weaver, a potter, a jeweler or buy an old-fashioned treat ("penny" candy or little Coca-Cola bottles) or toy at the General Store. Demonstrations of the works of a candle-maker, broom-maker, and blacksmith occur throughout the day. Many people enjoy the mule-drawn wagon rides through the village and surrounding area.

CECIL M. HARDEN LAKE STATE RESERVOIR

160 S. Raccoon Pkwy. (Raccoon State Recreation Area)

Rockville 47872

❑   Phone: (765) 344-1412
     Web: www.in.gov/dnr/parklake/reservoirs/cecil.html
❑   Admission: $3.00-$5.00 per vehicle. Swimming entrance extra.

Like to look for wildflowers, berries, nuts and mushrooms? Surrounded by dozens of species of trees, Harden Lake is a naturalist's delight. Other facilities are: Archery, Basketball Courts, Horseshoe Pits, Volleyball Courts, Camping, Fishing/Ice Fishing, Hiking Trails, Rentals-Fishing Boats/Pontoons, and Swimming / Beach.

OWEN-PUTNAM STATE FOREST

RR Box 214

Spencer 46460

❑   Phone: (812) 829-2462
     Web: www.state.in.us/dnr/forestry/property/owenput.htm

Hike through some of the best hardwood forests in the country. Enjoy deer, squirrel and turkey hunting. Fish in one of the many ponds. Horseback ride through some of the beautiful hills of south central Indiana, including a view of a 50-foot sandstone bluff.

MCCORMICK'S CREEK STATE PARK

Route 5, Box 282 (CR 46 near CR 43)

Spencer 47460

❑   Phone: (812) 829-2235
     Web: www.in.gov/dnr/parklake/parks/mccormickscreek.html
❑   Admission: $3.00-$5.00 per vehicle.

For updates visit our website: www.kidslovepublications.com

Canyon Inn (812) 829-4881 Accommodations, Restaurant and Pool. Unique limestone formations and scenic waterfalls along the White River. Hike through the thick wooded area or roam leisurely through the magnificent canyon surrounded by high cliffs. Also cabins, cultural programs, nature center and camping.

CHILDREN'S SCIENCE AND TECHNOLOGY MUSEUM

523 Wabash Avenue (downtown)

Terre Haute 47807

- ❑   Phone: (812) 235-5548, **Web: www.cstm.org**
- ❑   Hours: Tuesday-Saturday 9:00am - 4:00pm.
- ❑   Admission: $2.50 adult, $2.00 senior (65+), $2.00 child (3-12).

This small museum has hands-on science like: a shadow wall, lasers, a stoplight, model trains, holograms, fossils, a TV studio, marble races, a toddler play area and every changing "Slices of Americana" (play pretend).

HISTORICAL MUSEUM OF THE WABASH VALLEY

1411 South Sixth Street

Terre Haute 47807

- ❑   Phone: (812) 235-9717
     Web: http://web.indstate.edu/community/vchs/home.html
- ❑   Hours: Tuesday-Sunday 1:00-4:00 pm (February -December).
     Craft demonstrations and history films on Sunday.
- ❑   Admission: FREE

The recreated General Store, post office, schoolroom, dressmaker's shop, bedroom, parlor, nursery, and toy shop showcase Vigo County history. Terre Haute is the Birthplace of the Coca-Cola bottle. The museum has a large collection of original Coca-Cola artifacts.

SHADES STATE PARK
RR 1, Box 72 (SR 1, Off SR 47)

Waveland 47989

- ❑ Phone: (765) 435-2810
  Web: www.in.gov/dnr/parklake/parks/shades.html
- ❑ Hours: April-October.
- ❑ Admission: $3.00-$5.00 per vehicle.

A 2200 acre park with Sandstone cliffs and adjacent Pine Hills Nature Preserve. Primitive camping and peaceful hiking trails and canoeing along Sugar Creek.

Chapter 4
North Central Area

Our Favorites...

Kokomo Opalescent Glass

Amish Acres

Northern Indiana Center for History

Deutsch Kase Haus

South Bend Chocolate Company

Bonneyville Mill

Circus Hall of Fame

College Football Hall of Fame

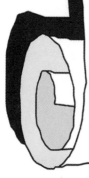

BONNEYVILLE MILL

53373 CR 131 (2 ½ miles East on SR120 to CR 131 South)

Bristol 46507

- ❑ Phone: (574) 535-6458, **Web: www.elkhartcountyparks.org**
- ❑ Hours: Daily 10:00am-5:00pm (May-October). Park grounds open year round.
- ❑ Admission: FREE
- ❑ Tours: Guided, weekdays, with reservation.
- ❑ Miscellaneous: Purchase freshly ground grains. Picnic area. Milling takes place on the half-hour.

See one of the oldest continually operating rustic gristmills in Indiana (1832). Watch as the miller grinds corn, wheat, buckwheat and rye using heavy milling stones. The freshly painted red mill and barn /gift shop is a delightful place to spend lunch. Beautiful park and walking trails are in the park, also.

ELKHART COUNTY MUSEUM

SR 120, 304 W. Vistula St. (Rush Memorial Center)

Bristol 46507

- ❑ Phone: (574) 848-4322, **Web: www.elkhartcounty.org**
- ❑ Hours: Tuesday-Friday 10:00am-4:00pm, Sunday 1:00-5:00pm (February-November). EST
- ❑ Admission: Donations accepted.

13 rooms include a Victorian row house, a one-room school, a train depot, a general store, a dentist, a barber, a pharmacy and a tool room. See one of the earliest toy trains made of cast iron or many authentic Native American tools and housewares.

NATIONAL NEW YORK CENTRAL RAILROAD MUSEUM

721 South Main Street (Right by Amtrak Railroad through town)

Elkhart 46514

- ❑ Phone: (574) 294-3001
- ❑ Hours: Tuesday-Friday 10:00am-2:00pm, Saturday 10:00am-4:00pm, Sunday Noon-4:00 pm.
- ❑ Admission: $2.00 adult, $1.00 senior (62+), $1.00 child (6-12).

Trace the railroad heritage of Elkhart through photos, videos of New York trains in action and two model railroad layouts in the 1880's Freight House Museum. Outside is a New York Central "Mohawk" steam locomotive that's very dark black and only slightly restored (it looks like it could tell lots of stories). There's also an E-8 Diesel and GG-1 Electric locomotive.

RIVER QUEEN

Bowers Court on St. Joseph's River (Off Jackson Boulevard)

Elkhart 46516

- ❑ Phone: (574) 522-1795
- ❑ Hours: Sundays 2:00pm (May-October)
- ❑ Admission: Around $5.00 per person.

Cruise up the St. Joseph River and learn fascinating facts about the river's history that dates back to 1841. Children like watching the ducks and other boats. At one time, the river was the only method of transportation.

RV/ MH HERITAGE MUSEUM
801 Benham Avenue
Elkhart 46516

❑   Phone: (574) 293-2344
      Web: www.rv-mh-hall-of-fame.org/museum.html
❑   Hours: Monday-Friday 9:00am-4:00pm. Open Saturdays (June-
      August). All other weekends by appointment. EST
❑   Admission: $3.00 per person, $10.00 per family.

History of RV and Manufactured Housing Industries showcased in
the National Hall of Fame, museum and library. See units from
1913-1960's. The units are displayed in a park-like setting with
life-size cutouts of characters in period dress. The museum also
presents chronological and technological advancements in the
industry from before WW I to the present.

GAS CITY I-69 SPEEDWAY
5739 East 500 South (I-69 exit 59)
Gas City 46933

❑   Phone: (765) 674-6135 or (765) 384-7285
      Web: www.gascityi69speedway.com
❑   Hours: Fridays at 7:30pm (May-October)
❑   Admission: $10.00 adult, $6.00 youth (13-15), $3.00 child (7-12),
      FREE child (6 and under)

Quarter mile dirt track, racing sprints, modified and street stock.

CITY OF FIRSTS AUTOMOTIVE MUSEUM
1500 N. Reed Rd (US 31 North, within the Johanning Civic Center)
Kokomo 46901

❑   Phone: (765) 454-9999 or (800) 837-0971
      Web: http://members.iquest.net/~deglen/automus.html

- ❑ Hours: Daily 10:00am-5:00pm. Closed Thanksgiving, Christmas, New Year's Day.
- ❑ Admission: Yes, children accompanied by adult are FREE.

The Museum has over 80 antique automobiles and automotive industry artifacts. Many autos, including several locally produced - and the first motorized fire engine can be seen and studied.

ELWOOD HAYNES MUSEUM

1915 South Webster Street (off US 31, follow signs)

Kokomo 46902

- ❑ Phone: (765) 456-7500
- ❑ Hours: Tuesday-Saturday 1:00-4:00pm, Sunday 1:00-5:00pm. Closed Holidays.
- ❑ Admission: FREE

Haynes' former residence houses many personal possessions and most interesting, his inventions (including 4 vintage Haynes cars). He invented "America's First Car" road tested July 4, 1894 on Pumpkinville Pike. See the first stellite cobalt-based alloy discovered in 1906. While searching for metal to make new tableware, Haynes in the same process, invented stainless steel. The tarnish-free dinnerware was developed to satisfy Mrs. Haynes' request.

KOKOMO OPALESCENT GLASS COMPANY

1310 South Market Street

Kokomo 46902

- ❑ Phone: (765) 457-1829 (tours), **Web: www.kog.com**
- ❑ Admission: FREE
- ❑ Tours: Wednesday and Friday at 10:00am (except holidays and the month of December) or by appointment. No sandals. Parents must stay with children.

❑   Miscellaneous: Broken glass everywhere so follow guide's
     instructions carefully. Gift shop. Hot Glass Studio produce a
     unique range of quality hand blown glass using the world famous
     Kokomo Opalescent glass.

Dating back to 1888, it is the only remaining "Gas Boom" factory
where up to 100 different types of glass are made for stained glass
artisans. Four ingredients are used: flint, phosphorus, sand and
opal – the combination is a secret known only by the owners. The
2400 degree furnaces run 365 days a year and 13 different roller
patterns are used (some are custom to Tiffany glass). The process
starts when the table guy rings the bell, the "ladlers" use giant
ladles to scoop out different colored molten glass and spoon it onto
the table where it's mixed with a giant fork. Next the blob is rolled,
slowly cooled and then cut. A pink color is expensive because it
contains some 24K gold. Red, orange and yellow are also
expensive because they contain arsenic (which is expensive to
ventilate during production). This tour is a big WOW!

CASS COUNTY CAROUSEL

1208 Riverside Drive

Logansport 46947

❑   Phone: (574) 753-8725
❑   Hours: Daily evenings and weekend afternoons (Summer).
     Weekends only (September-December).
❑   Admission: 50 cents/ride.

A restored, working Merry-Go-Round of 42 wooden animals hand-
carved by Gustav Dentzel (regarded as the finest carousel artist of
his kind) in 1896. The Brass Ring, Band Organ and kiddie train
add to the fun.

CASS COUNTY MUSEUM

1004 East Market Street (Jerolaman-Long House)

Logansport 46947

❑   Phone: (574) 753-3866
❑   Hours: Tuesday-Saturday 1:00-5:00pm (limited hours in the winter). First Monday of the month 1:00-7:00pm.
❑   Admission: FREE
❑   Miscellaneous: Civil War. American Indian including prints by artist, George Winters. Log Cabin and Barn with period furnishings.

DEUTSCH KASE HAUS

11275 W CR250 North (pronounced "Doytch Case House")

Middlebury 45640

❑   Phone: (574) 825-9511
❑   Hours: Monday-Friday, 8:00am-5:00pm. Phone ahead to be sure they are making cheese each day.
❑   Admission: FREE
❑   Tours: View easily through giant windows
❑   Miscellaneous: Retail shop also open Saturday 8:00 am-3:00 pm. Sample cheeses freshly made.

Making cheese is an art and this cheese haus takes no short cuts. They start with milk brought from Amish farms. The cows were milked the day before and the milk cooled in 10 gallon cans. Once at the cheese factory, the milk is pasteurized and placed in giant tubs where enzymes and flavors are added. Giant rotating stirrers (this is the favorite part to watch) separate the milk into whey and cheese curd. Later, the whey is drawn off and the remaining curd is salted and pressed. Our favorite cheese type they make is World Champion Colby - it really tastes better than any commercial brand (creamier, too!).

COACHMEN RV'S

423 North Main Street (SR 13 South)

Middlebury 46540

❑ Phone: (574) 825-5821, **Web: www.caravanatcoachmen.com**
❑ Admission: FREE
❑ Tours: Monday-Friday at 3:00pm. One hour long. Meet at
Visitors Center.

As you begin the tour, you'll drive up to the chassis storage area
(looks like the length of a football field). Now see that chassis built
into the familiar Coachmen Dalmatian-logoed RV's. Cranes lift,
saws buzz, and workers tediously wire and install equipment.
Learn about their "rain booth" that exposes the finished vehicle to
storm conditions (reveals any leaks).

DAS DUTCHMAN ESSENHAUS

240 US 20 (1 mile West of SR 13)

Middlebury 46540

❑ Phone: (574) 825-9471 or (800) 455-9471
Web: www.essenhaus.com
❑ Hours: Daily 6:00am-8:00 or 9:00pm (except Sunday). Farm
open 9:00am-7:00pm (Spring-Fall, weather permitting). Closed
Thanksgiving, Christmas and New Years.
❑ Admission: Farm - $5.25 per person (age 2+).

Buggy rides along carriage trails and through a covered bridge are
available while you wait for your table. The Amish Country Decor
restaurant complex includes a bakery, candymakers, and Amish
crafts. Kids like the Sunshine Farm & Mini-golf area with
miniature horses, sheep, milking goats and baby chickens.

JAYCO RECREATIONAL VEHICLES

58075 SR 13 South (SR 13, just south of US 20)

Middlebury 46540

❑　Phone: (574) 825-5861 (ask for Visitor Center)
  Web: www.jayco.com
❑　Admission: FREE
❑　Tours: Approximately 1 1/2 hours total. Monday-Friday at
  1:30pm. Also at 9:30am (June-August). Closed holidays, 4th of
  July week and week between Christmas and New Years.
❑　Miscellaneous: Groups of 10+ should call for reservations. The
  Visitor Center has historical memorabilia and a gift shop.

Deep in Amish Country, this company employs the work of mostly
Amish and their dedication to quality is evident as you travel
through the factory. Begin the tour watching a video about the
history and production methods of this company, then, on to the
floor where you'll see their towable travel trailers made from
beginning to end. Starting as a tubular steel frame, wood flooring,
sidewalls, carpeting, cabinets and appliances are then added. Lots
of wood and metal are used and finally the roof is bolted on.

HANNAH LINDHAL CHILDREN'S MUSEUM

1402 South Main Street

Mishawaka 46544

❑　Phone: (574) 254-4540, **Web: www.hlcm.org**
❑　Hours: Tuesday-Friday 9:00am-4:00pm (during school year).
  Tuesday-Thursday 10:00am-2:00pm (June). Closed July and
  August and all school holidays.
❑　Admission: $1.00 general (age 6+), $0.50 child (2-5)
❑　Miscellaneous: Survive Alive! Fire Safety demos with real
  firemen (mornings only).

The theme is "Please Do Touch" and kids' eye-level, hands-on
exhibits focus on the geological history of the area from glaciers to
the early 1900's. Touch different surfaces that were affected by the

glaciers. View Native American artifacts, tools, clothing, and tee-pees. A Japanese theme room (try on an outfit!) and mid-1800's street, too.

AMISH ACRES

1600 West Market Street (US 6 off SR 19 or I-69 exit US 6 west, follow signs)

Nappanee 46550

❑ Phone: (800) 800-4942 or (574) 773-4188
   Web: www.amishacres.com
❑ Hours: Daily 10:00am - 6:00 or 7:00pm (late March-December). Closed Mondays in November & December. Open Friday-Sunday in March.
❑ Admission: Varies with attraction. $3.95-$8.95 adult ($25.00 for theatre show, $15.45 Dinner), $1.95-$4.95 child ($6.00 for theatre show or Threshers Dinner).
❑ Miscellaneous: Village shops open until 5:00 pm. Summertime lunches available. The Round Barn Theater "Plain and Fancy" musical comedy is about Amish culture and pop culture intertwined. If you've seen this production, check out one of their other off-Broadway style productions (shows 10 months per year). Evening shows at 8:00pm, matinees at 2:00pm. See website for schedule.

After you watch a documentary film, tour a 122 year Amish homestead where the family still clings to simple dress and gentle farming. See chores and crafts of a typical Amish family including gardens, orchards and livestock. The village was restored to historical accuracy by Amish craftsmen. It features a long, narrow farmhouse, a grossdaadi house-for the extended family, and attendant outbuildings, all original on site. In addition, eleven restored structures have been brought to Amish Acres from across the county, including a sawmill, an ice house, a mint still, and an authentic Amish blacksmith shop. Take a buggy ride and countryside tour. You'll have built up your appetite for the Thresher's Dinner at the Restaurant Barn. It's a thirteen item dinner full of family style food (our favorite is the first course including flavored pickles, apple butter and bean soup). If you're trying new foods, order shoo-fly pie for dessert (only if you LOVE the taste of molasses).

POTATO CREEK STATE PARK

25601 SR 4

North Liberty 46554

❏   Phone: (574) 656-8186
    Web: www.state.in.us/dnr/parklake/parks/potatocreek.html
❏   Admission: $3.00-$5.00 per vehicle.

3840 acres with beach, boat/bike rental, paved trails, family campground, horseman's campground, general store and nature center and exhibits. A variety of natural habitats await the visitor to this park including the 327 acre Worster Lake, old fields, mature woodlands, restored prairies and diverse wetlands offering opportunities for plant and wildlife observations. Cabins and camping (with reservations), too.

CIRCUS HALL OF FAME

SR 124 (3 miles East of Peru @ Wallace Circus Winter Center, US 31Bus east, right on Main, right on Rt. 19, left on SR 124)

Peru 46970

❏   Phone: (765) 472-7553 or (800) 771-0241
    Web: www.circushalloffame.com
❏   Hours: Monday-Saturday 10:00am-5:00pm, Sunday 1:00-5:00pm (mid-June to Labor Day)
❏   Admission: $10.00 adult, $9.00 senior, $8.00 youth (6-12), $4.00 (4 & 5 yr. Olds), FREE (age 3 and under)
❏   Miscellaneous: "Summer only" (mid-June to mid-August) performances (twice daily) include calliope concerts, magic circus, animal training and Big Top Circus Shows. Gift Shop.

If you want to see the best of circus life today and days gone-by, you need to go to the source of the most activity in the last 200 years. As you pull up, you'll see the bright Big Top and the sounds of animals and their trainers yelling out commands. In between shows throughout the grounds (see Miscellaneous above), stop over to the Circus Museum. It's located in an old circus barn that served as winter quarters for up to 5 famous traveling shows. Going through the Hall of Fame, you'll recognize greats like Emmett Kelly (classic 1900's clown) and Dan Rice (his act was the character Uncle Sam clown). Our favorites in the museum were the vintage circus wagons, painted colorfully inside and out with closets full of even more brightly colorful costumes.

GRISSOM AIR MUSEUM

US 31 (6500 Hoosier Boulevard next to Grissom Air Reserve Base)

Peru 46970

❑ Phone: (765) 688-2654, **Web: www.grissomairmuseum.com**
❑ Hours: Tuesday-Saturday 10:00am-4:00pm. Closed mid-December - February and Holidays.
❑ Admission: FREE
❑ Miscellaneous: Theater. Gift Shop.

The outdoor display includes the B-17 Flying Fortress (as if still on alert on a green English airfield), the sleek, fast B-58 Hustler and the fighter A-10 Warthog - plus 12 more planes. Inside the museum, visitors can sit in the cockpit of a Phantom jet, view a flight trainer, see displays of uniforms, models, survival gear (very interesting), and plane instruments. If weather permits, take the time to climb the tall tower outside and get a "birds-eye" view of the airplanes on display and planes landing and taking off from the base airport.

MIAMI COUNTY MUSEUM

51 North Broadway (Downtown, US 24 and US 31)

Peru 46970

- ❑   Phone: (765) 473-9183, **Web: www.netusa1.net/~mchs**
- ❑   Hours: Tuesday-Saturday 9:00am-5:00pm
- ❑   Admission: $2.00 suggested donation.
- ❑   Tours: By appointment

A local history museum containing artifacts relative to Miami Indians, trading posts, circuses, Cole Porter (composer and song writer) hometown tribute with display of his Grammy and 1955 Fleetwood Cadillac. Drug store, dentist office, penny scales, and quarter player piano.

MISSISSINEWA LAKE STATE RESERVOIR

4763 S. 625E

Peru 46970

- ❑   Phone: (765) 473-6528

  www.state.in.us/dnr/parklake/reservoirs/mississinewa.html
- ❑   Admission: $3.00-$5.00 per vehicle.

Features include: Basketball Court, Horseshoes, Volleyball, Frisbee Golf Course, Radio Controlled Flying Field, camping, fishing and boating, and a swimming / beach.

MARSHALL COUNTY HISTORICAL MUSEUM

123 N. Michigan Street

Plymouth 46563

- ❑   Phone: (574) 936-2306

  www.blueberrycountry.org/attractions/countymuseum.html

❑ Hours: Tuesday-Friday 9:00am-5:00pm, Saturday 10:00am-
    4:00pm. Closed all county holidays.
❑ Admission: Donations accepted.

Marshall County has a museum located in the historic Lauer Building in downtown Plymouth. The museum serves as a showcase for the county. The main floor is a changing gallery with thematic exhibits. Upstairs, some of the former offices which were occupied by early doctors, lawyers, etc. have been converted to scenarios which depict life in the area between 1870 and 1910. There is a bedroom, kitchen, parlor and a child's bedroom with furnishings of the time periods. You can even visit an old time general store where Mrs. Thayer is purchasing eggs.. Other theme rooms include: A woodworking room, complete with a log cabin front; A textile room containing fashions and trim from bygone eras; The agricultural room has the tools of the farmer's trade. Plows, planters and cultivators show how hard it was to "live on the land."; A doctor's office contains all of the essentials of the medical arts; and, another unique room reflects the importance of the church in the lives of the county's residents. A chapel is set up with carved oak pulpit chairs, a portable organ and a handmade communion altar.

FULTON COUNTY MUSEUM AND VILLAGE

37 East 375 North (Tippecanoe River and US 31 North)

Rochester 46975

❑ Phone: (574) 223-4436, **Web: www.icss.net/~fchs**
❑ Hours: Monday-Saturday 9:00am-5:00pm
❑ Admission: FREE
❑ Miscellaneous: Gift Shop. Indian and American apparel and toys.

This county is the "Round Barn Capitol of the World" and a central part of your visit is a restored 1924 round barn museum with farm machinery and tools. The museum also features themed rooms like Homes, Toys, Hospitals, Indians, Transportation, General Stores, Schools and Sports, Military, Recreation, Business, Churches, and the Circus. Each room gives you information on little known facts. Another extra touch is the Living History Village called "Loyal, Indiana" where you walk from the depot to a jail, log cabin, blacksmith shop, stagecoach inn, print shop and windmill & cider mill. The village is only open on Saturdays and during Festivals, except during the summer when it is open when the museum is open.

UNIVERSITY OF NOTRE DAME

111 Ecks Visitors Center

South Bend 46556

❑   Phone: (574) 631-5726, **Web: www.nd.edu/~eckvisit**
❑   Hours: Monday-Saturday 8:00am-5:00pm, Sunday 11:00am-5:00pm.
❑   Tours: Monday-Friday 10:00am-3:00pm.

Official welcome center for the University of Notre Dame is the starting point to begin a walking tour of the mystical campus founded in 1842. Watch the 12 minute DVD highlighting some history and fame, then look for notable landmarks like the Snite Museum of Art, the "Golden Dome", the Grotto and Log Chapel. Be sure to include the "Fighting Irish" football grounds and a snack at "Reckers" (South Hall) food court.

COLLEGE FOOTBALL HALL OF FAME

111 South St. Joseph Street (Downtown, 2 blocks East of Main Street, off US 31 or I-80/90 exit 77)

South Bend 46601

❑   Phone: (574) 235-9999, (800) 440 FAME
    Web: www.collegefootball.org
❑   Hours: Daily 10:00am-5:00pm (January-May). Daily 10:00am-7:00pm (June-December). Closed Thanksgiving, Christmas and New Years. Extended hours during weekends of Notre Dame home football games.

❑   Admission: $10.00 adult, $7.00 senior (62+), $4.00 child (6-14)
❑   Miscellaneous: Gift shop-logo and autographed items.

- **THE LOCKER ROOM** - Walk into a scene where coaches are training and motivating future football heroes. Designed to make you feel you're really being coached.
- **PIGSKIN PAGEANTRY** - interactive tribute to the fans, mascots, cheerleaders and marching bands that create the festivity.
- **HALL OF CHAMPIONS** - photos and mementos.
- **STADIUM THEATER** – 360 degree screen theater that puts you in the middle of a game from pre-game cheers, to playing rough on the field, to the victory celebration.
- **TRAINING CENTER/PRACTICE FIELD** – Test YOUR football skills at a series of challenges in passing, running, and kicking.

Even as you walk up to the building, your kids will have fun playing on the ½ football field entrance (we bought a College Football Hall of Fame football and later played catch on "the turf" outside). See the "Pursuit of a Dream" (college football theme sculpture - 3 stories tall!) that will be reminiscent for any college grad (can you count the # of pizza boxes?).

HEALTHWORKS! KIDS MUSEUM

111 W. Jefferson, Suite 200 (2nd Floor Memorial Leighton HealthPlex)

South Bend 46601

❑   Phone: (574) 287-5437
    Web: www.qualityoflife.org/healthworks.htm
❑   Hours: Tuesday-Friday 9:00am-5:00pm, Saturday Noon-5:00pm.
❑   Admission: $5.00 adult, $3.00 child (2-17).

They're putting health habits into play! The center is designed to help children understand that the choices they make today will have an impact on the quality of their lives tomorrow. The museum offers a wide variety of hands-on exhibit areas unlocking the mysteries of the human body. When you visit HealthWorks! you will see: Bodyworks!, The Main Brain (go in to a nine year olds brain!), MindWorks! Brain challenges, All About Me, Interactive Learning Theaters and lots of colorful, engaging fun spaces.

NORTHERN INDIANA CENTER FOR HISTORY

808 West Washington Street

South Bend 46601

- ❑ Phone: (574) 235-9664, **Web: www.centerforhistory.org**
- ❑ Hours: Tuesday-Saturday 10:00am-5:00pm, Sunday Noon-5:00pm. Groups by appointment. Closed all major holidays.
- ❑ Admission: $5.00-$10.00 adult, $4.00-$8.00 senior (60+), $3.00-$4.50 depending on number of activities.
- ❑ Tours: Copshaholm, a Victorian mansion of founders of Oliver Chilled Plow Works and a factory Workers Home are on or near the premises to tour.
- ❑ Miscellaneous: Gift Shop - mostly decorative items. Memberships available.

HISTORY CENTER - Discover legends of the St. Joseph River valley from explorer LaSalle to industrialist Joseph Oliver. Explore Notre Dame's history, pick up phones, push buttons or play a circular table board game of Agronomy. Other highlights were the All American Girls Baseball League displaying uniforms of the South Bend Blue Sox along with actual photos of team members. The "girls" were coached to be extremely feminine while playing the game (this during World War II when pro baseball was cancelled due to lack of male players). See examples of major manufacturing companies in the area, too (ex. honey, mint production).

KIDS FIRST CHILDREN'S MUSEUM - The large open room takes children on a trip along St. Joseph's River. From Native American dwellings (good picture opportunities of kids sitting in a canoe dressing in costumes, trading furs, tracking animals or relaxing in a wig-wam)…to agriculture (become a worm and slide on a dirt hill), to the industrial boom. Here you pretend you're an assembly line worker using wheels, cranks and buttons to learn how locally grown mint is processed. Very creative pretend fun!

SILVER HAWKS BASEBALL
501 West South Street (Coveleski Regional Stadium)
South Bend 46601

- ❑   Phone: (574) 235-9988, **Web: www.silverhawks.com**
- ❑   Season: May - August.
- ❑   Admission: $5.00-$7.00 adult, $3.00 child/senior.

Class "A" baseball team for the Arizona Diamondbacks. Look for Swoop, Kids Club specials, the newer FunZone at the stadium or Dollar Mondays.

SOUTH BEND REGIONAL MUSEUM OF ART
120 South St. Joseph Street (Century Center)
South Bend 46601

- ❑   Phone: (574) 235-9102, **Web: www.sbt.infi.net/~sbrma/**
- ❑   Hours: Tuesday-Friday 11:00am-5:00pm, Saturday-Sunday Noon-5:00pm. Extended hours til 7:00pm on the "First Friday" of each month.
- ❑   Admission: $3.00 suggested donation.

An Arts Education Center with classes and galleries focusing on American Art with a regional flare. Mostly regional works with a strong sculpture emphasis.

SOUTH BEND SYMPHONY ORCHESTRA

120 West LaSalle (various locations in the area)

South Bend 46601

❑   Phone: (574) 239-7788, **Web: www.sbsymphony.org**
❑   Miscellaneous: Firefly Festival for the Performing Arts is held
    each summer (mid-June thru early August) with all kinds of
    concerts, food and dance to explore - www.fireflyfestival.com.

Music lovers can enjoy concerts offering six Masterworks, three
POPS!, two family, three chamber and a holiday concert. Side-by-
Side Concert showcases gifted high school musicians playing
alongside seasoned Symphony veterans.

STUDEBAKER NATIONAL MUSEUM

525 South Main Street (Downtown. Off SR 2 or US 31)

South Bend 46601

❑   Phone: (574) 235-9714 or (888) 391-5600
    Web: www.studebakermuseum.org
❑   Hours: Monday-Saturday 9:00am-5:00pm, Sunday Noon-5:00
    pm. Closed Mondays (November-March) and Easter,
    Thanksgiving, Christmastime and New Years.
❑   Admission: $5.50 adult, $4.50 senior (60+) and student (over 12),
    $3.00 child (under 12).
❑   Miscellaneous: Gift Shop and Science Center Gift Shop. X90
    Hands On Science and Technology Center features pulleys and
    fasteners using principles applicable to vehicle mechanics.

Two Studebaker brothers started supplying wagons to the US
Army for the Civil War and then later WWI. Then four brothers
formed a company that grew to be the largest wagon factory in the
world. Their motto was, "Always give more than you promise". By
the 1920's, they were building electric and gasoline-powered
automobiles and continued until closing in 1966. (They were the
only company that built settlers' wagons all the way up to high
performance autos). See the family's Conestoga wagon, a platinum

1934 Bendix and the last car ever made in South Bend. There's also an impressive display of carriages belonging to Presidents Grant, McKinley and Lincoln. The one and only white Packard Predictor is in the entrance enclosed in a temperature-controlled case. Can you guess why it has to be in its own case?

EAST RACE WATERWAY

301 South St. Louis Blvd. (along Niles Ave. & Jefferson Blvd.)

South Bend 46615

❑ Phone: (574) 235-9328 or (574) 235-9401

A 2000 ft. artificial whitewater course with canoe and kayak national and international races and open to public. (June - Labor Day). The first artificial whitewater course in North America is a place where Beginners to Advanced adventurers can ride funyacks for 1 or 2 people or whitewater rafts for 2 to 6 people.

SOUTH BEND CHOCOLATE COMPANY

3300 West Sample Street (just West of downtown. Off US 31)

South Bend 46619

❑ Phone: (574) 233-2577 or (800) 301-4961
   Web: www.sbchocolate.com
❑ Admission: FREE
❑ Tours: Factory: By appointment, Monday-Friday. Chocolate Store & Lobby displays/Self-Tour: Monday-Friday 8:30am-5:00pm or Saturday 9:00am-2:00pm. Closed major holidays.
❑ Miscellaneous: Exhibits and film of chocolate making process in Foyer. Free treat (bag full of goodies) at the end of the tour.

From the minute you walk up to the front door, you'll be surrounded with the smell of chocolate (they use cocoa bean shells as mulch in their plant beds outside!). Even the waiting area is fun with "chocolate-related" films playing (i.e. Willie Wonka) and little known facts like cocoa beans were once used as currency.

The real fun treat before the tour is to adorn your complimentary white hair net and stand by a scaled-down conveyor just like the one Lucy and Ethel used (their picture with mouthfuls of candy is in the background). You must get a picture of this! The tour is simple and short and includes the "chocolate waterfall" and viewing a 10 lb. candy bar. Look for funny named treats like the DOMER, ROCKNE and NUTS FOR ND. As their sticker says, "You'll be sweeter since you visited South Bend Chocolate Company".

SOUTH BEND MOTOR SPEEDWAY

25698 State Road 2

South Bend 46619

❑   Phone: (574) 287-1704
     Web: www.southbendmotorspeedway.com
❑   Hours: Fridays & Saturdays beginning at 7:00pm (qualifying)
     and 8:00pm (races) (April-September).

Demolition Derby, auto stock racing, formula Indy, classic stock, and IMCA modified.

OLD WAKARUSA RAILROAD COME AND DINE RESTAURANT

66402 SR 19 (Indiana Toll Road to SR 19 South - 13 miles)

Wakarusa 46573

❑   Phone: (574) 862-2714
❑   Hours: Daily, except Monday 11:00 am-Dark. (Railroad: April-
     December only). Sunday Brunch served, no dinner.
❑   Admission: $5.00 per run for train rides. Moderate prices for
     meals.

A one and one-half mile ride on a 1/3 replica of the famous General Locomotive past a "mini-village". You'll start by going under an overpass, then past a miniature water tower, over low hills, past a small lake, through a long tunnel and even intersect one stretch of a local street. With everything miniature, it's just the right size for your little ones and s-o-o-o cute to watch and ride! Our kids each got an engineer's cap (pink for girls and blue for boys) which added to the excitement. The Restaurant features Amish country cooking with a bakery and gift shop. While waiting for your train ride, look at the antique tractor display outside.

HOLIDAY RAMBLER & MONACO COACH RV'S

606 Nelsons Pkwy. (Monaco Site) (1722 Mishawaka Road - Holiday Rambler site)

Wakarusa/Elkhart 46573/46517

❑ Phone: (800) 650-7337 (Monaco) or (800) 866-6226 (Rambler) **Web: www.monacocoach.com**
❑ Admission: FREE
❑ Tours: Approximately two hours total. Monday-Friday 10:00am and 2:00pm at either location. Closed holidays, week between Christmas and New Years, and first two weeks of July.

Children (at least age 2+, no strollers please) and their adults can visit the factory floor to watch the construction of motorized and towable RV's. Highlights of the frame construction (lightweight, yet durable) including studding, welding, joining, riveting and paneling can be seen.

KOSCIUSKO COUNTY JAIL MUSEUM

121 North Indiana Street (corner of Main & Indiana)

Warsaw 46580

❑ Phone: (574) 269-1078, **Web: http://culture.kconline.com/kchs**
❑ Hours: Thursday-Saturday 9:00am-4:00pm, Sunday 1:00-4:00pm.
❑ Admission: Donation

The white stone building served as a public jail from 1871-1982. Nostalgic items are displayed in renovated jail cells and sheriff's living quarters.

WAGON WHEEL THEATRE

2517 E. Center Street

Warsaw 46580

❑   Phone: (574) 267-8041

Wagon Wheel Theatre is a privately owned theatre-in-the-round that has become one of the most popular summer theatres in the Midwest. From the first summer, in a tent in 1956, to the current 838-seat, air-conditioned building, area theatre-goers have seen In-the-Round stage performances of children's and family productions. During winter months, audiences enjoy popular performing artists.

WARSAW BIBLICAL GARDENS

313 South Buffalo (SR 15 North at Canal Street)

Warsaw 46580

❑   Phone: (574) 267-6419, **Web: www.warsawbiblicalgardens.org**
❑   Hours: Dawn to dusk (mid-April to mid-October)
❑   Admission: FREE

The largest of five such gardens in the U.S., this offers an oasis of beauty, education, joy, and contemplation for all. It is open to all people, regardless of race, faith, creed or physical capabilities. The ¾ acre garden contains trees, flowers, herbs and plants mentioned in the Bible.

WARSAW CUT GLASS COMPANY

505 S. Detroit Street

Warsaw 46580

❑   Phone: (574) 267-6581 or (574) 269-5166
❑   Hours: Monday - Saturday 9:00am - 5:00pm
❑   Admission: FREE

❑   Tours: Of showroom and manufacturing facility during business hours. Watch cutting - 10:00am or 2:00pm (best times if group). No tours November and December.

Using turn-of-the century machinery, artisans hand cut pieces of clear crystal using techniques of the early 1900's. Stone wheels run with leather belts in a 1911 vintage workshop.

BILLY SUNDAY HOME

101 Fourth Street (Park Avenue to 12th Street)

Winona Lake 46590

❑   Phone: (574) 268-9888 or (877) 786-3292
❑   Hours: Monday-Saturday 8:00am-5:00pm. Hours do vary seasonally. Please call first.
❑   Admission: $1.00 (Donation)
❑   Tours: By appointment.

Reveals the life of "Ma" and Billy Sunday from the days of his evangelistic crusades to a pro baseball career (uniform and mitt). Listen to a real victrola.

Chapter 5
North East Area

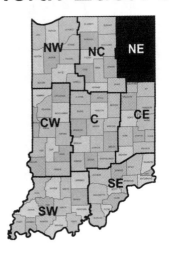

Lincoln Museum

Sechler's Fine Pickles

Menno-Hof

Amishville USA

Amish Dressup Tour

BLACK PINE ANIMAL PARK

349 West Albion Road (US 33 to SR9 north)

Albion 46701

- ❏ Phone: (260) 636-7383, **Web: www.blackpineanimalpark.com**
- ❏ Hours: Summers only except special events throughout the year. Tuesday-Saturday 10:00am-4:00pm, Sunday 1:00-4.00pm. Weekends only in May and October.
- ❏ Admission: $5.00 adult, $4.00 senior (55+) or child (3-12).
- ❏ Miscellaneous: Feeding tour on Saturday / Sunday at 4:00 pm is $1.00 additional.

Animals from around the world which are rescued, rehabilitated or have retired from show business are sent here. A unique opportunity to meet (REALLY up-close!) exotic and endangered animals like lions, tigers, chimpanzees, monkeys, bears, and dozens of other mammals, birds, and reptiles from all over the world. Both short and longer, educational tours are available, or, just wander around.

CHAIN O'LAKES STATE PARK

2355 East 75 South (off SR 9)

Albion 46701

- ❏ Phone: (260) 636-2654
  Web: www.in.gov/dnr/parklake/parks/chainolakes.html
- ❏ Admission: $3.00-$5.00 per vehicle.

Eight connecting lakes are the focus here with boating/canoeing, hiking trails or attending a nature program in the park's "Old Schoolhouse" Nature Center. A beach seasonally provides swimming. Cabins, camping and fishing/ice fishing, too.

SALAMONIE LAKE STATE RESERVOIR

9214 West Lost Bridge West (off Rte. 524 or SR 124)

Andrews 46702

❑ Phone: (260) 468-2125 or (260) 468-2127 Nature Center
❑ Admission: $3.00-$5.00 per vehicle.

Tons of facilities are available here for outdoor adventure: Bridle Trails, Basketball and Volleyball on beach, Cross-country skiing, Snowmobile Trails, Boating & Marina, 246 Modern Campsites, 210 Primitive Campsites, 40 Horsemen's Campsites, Cultural Arts Programs, Fishing, Hiking Trails, Model Airport, Swimming/ Beach, State Forest, and a nicely remodeled Nature Center. The Center has interpretive programs, both indoors and out. The Indiana DNR recently reintroduced river otters into the Salamonie Reservoir area. Wild turkeys have also been reintroduced.

FUN SPOT PARK AND ZOO

2365 North Highway 200 West

Angola 46703

❑ Phone: (260) 833-2972 or (888) 534-8421
Web: www.funspotpark.com
❑ Hours: Daily 10:00am-10:00pm (Memorial-Labor Day)
❑ Admission: $13.00 adult (includes waterslides), $8.00 junior (under 48"), $3.00 general, FREE (age 2 and under)

Their rides include: Afterburner (largest in Indiana), Zyklon, Waterslides, Troika, Bayern Kurve, Sea Dragon, Paratrooper, Flying Scooters, Tilt-a-Whirl, Ferris Wheel, Scrambler, Roundup, Merry Go Round, Glass House, Bumper Cars, Go Karts, 12 Kiddie Rides. The zoo has ostrich, lemur, llamas and porcupines! Also mini-golf and arcades.

POKAGON STATE PARK

450 Lane 100, Lake James

Angola 46703

❑   Phone: (260) 833-2012

       Web: www.state.in.us/dnr/parklake/parks/pokagon.htm

❑   Admission: $3.00-$5.00 per vehicle.

Potawatomi Inn. (219) 833-1077. Accommodations & Restaurant, Swimming / Beach, Indoor Pool/Whirlpool, Boating, Tennis, Hiking, Cross-country skiing, and a Toboggan Run operating Thanksgiving Day through February with track speeds of 35-40 mph. Check out their Nature Center, too.

AUBURN-CORD DUESENBERG MUSEUM

1600 S. Wayne Street (I-69 exit SR 8)

Auburn 46706

❑   Phone: (260) 925-1444, **Web: www.acdmuseum.org**

❑   Hours: Daily 9:00am-5:00pm. Closed Thanksgiving, Christmas & New Years.

❑   Admission: $7.00 adult, $4.50 student. Family rates.

❑   Miscellaneous: Duesy gift shop.

America's showcase of classic cars fill the 1930 art deco showrooms of the former Auburn Automobile Company. Some 100 antique, vintage, classic and special-interest cars, from horseless carriages of the 19th century to muscle cars of the present, fill the two floors of the building. Learn how the innovative cars made their mark on our automobile industry.

NATIONAL TRUCK AND AUTOMOTIVE MUSEUM OF THE U.S. (NATMUS)

1000 Gordon M. Buehrig Place (adjacent to Auburn-Cord Museum)

Auburn 46706

- ❑ Phone: (260) 925-9100, **Web: www.natmus.org**
- ❑ Hours: Daily 9:00am-5:00pm. Closed Thanksgiving, Christmas and New Years
- ❑ Admission: $4.50 adult, $2.00 students (5-12)

The Museum focuses on post-WWII automobiles, trucks and engines of all years, and automotive toys and models. Over 1,000 automotive exhibits and thousands of toys and models are on display. A special exhibit features 50-year-old vehicles and memorabilia.

PINE LAKE WATER PARK

4640 W. SR 218

Berne 46711

- ❑ Phone: (260) 334-5649
- ❑ Hours: Monday-Saturday 10:00am-8:00pm, Sunday Noon-8:00pm (Memorial Day - Labor Day)
- ❑ Admission: Yes

Experience a full day of water fun with slides, platforms, cable ride, paddle boats, beach, volleyball, tennis, basketball and Concessions. Sand sculpture competition in July.

SWISS HERITAGE VILLAGE

1200 Swiss Way (off 500 South and SR 27. Follow signs)

Berne 46711

- ❑ Phone: (260) 589-8007, **Web: www.swissheritage.org**
- ❑ Hours: Monday-Saturday 9:00am-4:00 pm. (May-October)

For updates visit our website: www.kidslovepublications.com

❏   Admission: $4.00 adult, $2.00 students.

As you enter the town of Berne, you instantly know it seems like another country. Almost all of the buildings in town on SR 27 have a "Swiss look" to their store fronts. The village has fifteen historic buildings moved to one site. The Mill has the world's largest cider press. Have you ever wondered what it would be like to live in a farmhouse where there's no electricity, central heat or running water? Or what it took to turn cream into cheese? Maybe you'd like to attend an early Mennonite Church service or recite your lessons in a one-room country school? This, and other interesting facts are presented as you take the living history tours.

OUBACHE STATE PARK

4930 East SR 201

Bluffton 46714

❏   Phone: (260) 824-0926
     Web: www.in.gov/dnr/parklake/parks/ouabache.html
❏   Admission: $3.00-$5.00 per vehicle.

On the Wabash River. Swimming Pool with Waterslide, Tennis and Basketball Courts. Ouabache is difficult to spell, but easy to pronounce. Simply say "Wabash"...just like the river that forms the southwest boundary for the park. This is the French spelling of an Indian word, so don't be surprised to hear some folks call it o-ba-chee. Kunkel Lake offers excellent fishing. Other facilities include: Bicycle Trails, Boating, Camping, Cross-country Skiing (no rentals), Cultural Arts Programs, Hiking Trails, Naturalist services (seasonal, summer), Rental-Canoe, Paddleboat, Rowboat, Swimming / Pool / Waterslide, and Tennis / Basketball & Sand Volleyball Courts.

FOELLINGER-FREIMANN BOTANICAL CONSERVATORY

1100 South Calhoun Street (near Jefferson Street, downtown)

Fort Wayne 46802

- ❑ Phone: (260) 427-6440, **Web: www.botanicalconservatory.org**
- ❑ Hours: Monday-Saturday 10:00am-5:00pm, Sunday Noon-4:00pm. Closed Christmas.
- ❑ Admission: $3.00 adult, $2.00 child (4-14).

Even the lobby invites you to a tropical paradise as you browse over your map. Stop in the Tulip Tree Gift Shop that entices you to escape the stone and brick of the city for "gardens under glass". Their showcase display has changing seasons (mums in the Fall, Poinsettias at the Holidays, daffodils in the Spring) along with the permanent Desert House and Tropical House. Did you know a banana tree bears fruit once and then dies?

FORT WAYNE CIVIC THEATRE/ YOUTHTHEATRE

303 East Main Street (5220 Performing Arts Center)

Fort Wayne 46802

- ❑ Phone: (260) 422-8641or (260) 424-5220 box office or (219) 422-6900, **Web: www.fwcivic.org**
- ❑ Admission: Average $20.00 adult, Average $15.00 senior, $10.00 child (2-23)

The Civic Theater performs a wide range of scripts, from Shakespeare to contemporary comedy. Examples are "The Sound of Music" and Christmas-themed plays.

FORT WAYNE MUSEUM OF ART

311 East Main Street

Fort Wayne 46802

- ❑ Phone: (260) 422-6467, **Web: www.fwmoa.org**
- ❑ Hours: Tuesday-Saturday 10:00am-5:00pm, Sunday Noon-5:00 pm
- ❑ Admission: $3.00 adult, $2.00 student, $8.00 family. Free admission every Wednesday and on the first Sunday of the month.

Contemporary art. A special hands-on education gallery makes learning about art a fun experience for youngsters.

LINCOLN MUSEUM

200 E. Berry Street (I-69 to SR 14)

Fort Wayne 46802

- ❑ Phone: (260) 455-3864, **Web: www.thelincolnmuseum.org**
- ❑ Hours: Tuesday-Saturday 10:00am-5:00pm, Sunday 1:00-5:00pm. Closed New Years Day, Easter, Memorial Day, July 4th, Labor Day, Thanksgiving, Christmas.
- ❑ Admission: $2.99 adult, $1.99 senior (60+) and child (5-12). Notice your "souvenir" penny change when paying admission.
- ❑ Miscellaneous: Theaters and Museum Shops

The world's largest privately-owned Lincoln collection is based on the theme (in the words of Lincoln), "Most governments have been based, practically, on the denial of equal rights of men. Ours began, by affirming those rights." A wonderfully presented museum, it takes you through the political life of Lincoln and his family. The first thing we were struck by were the numerous pictures / paintings of Lincoln without a beard--can you imagine? Interactive exhibits included the War Department telegraph room (plan Civil War strategies - what would you do?), a touch screen that lets you pretend you're Mr. and Mrs. Lincoln reading mail, or modern day Lincoln Logs (1000's of them) to play with. Favorites are also the display of Lincoln's favorite songs, cake and friends or the "Dear Mr. Lincoln" desk where kids write letters to the President. A recent and important museum acquisition is a rare edition of The Emancipation Proclamation, signed by Lincoln in 1864.

OLD CITY HALL HISTORICAL MUSEUM

302 East Berry Street (Downtown, behind the Lincoln Museum)

Fort Wayne 46802

❑   Phone: (260) 426-2882
❑   Hours: Tuesday-Friday 10:00am-5:00pm, Saturday-Sunday
        Noon-5:00pm. (Closed January)
❑   Admission: $2.00 adult, $1.00 student, $5.00 family.

Explore the history of Allen County in the 100 year old sandstone city hall (looks like a castle). Favorites include the 1880's Street of Shops and the 1886 dollhouse. Go back further in time to the 1700's clash of Native Americans and early settlers (see Little Turtle's personal belongings and Anthony Wayne's camp bed). Before you leave, pretend to "do time" in the city jail or take a look at 1900's inventions created in Allen County or Indiana.

CORVETTE CLASSICS

6702 Point Inverness Way (I-69 exit 105B, Illinois Rd., then west on SR 14, then left on Hadley Road)

Fort Wayne 46804

❑   Phone: (260) 436-3444, **Web: www.corvette-classics.com**
❑   Hours: Monday-Friday 10:00am-6:00pm, Saturday 10:00am-
        5:00pm, Sunday Noon-5:00pm.
❑   Admission: $5.00 per person.

Corvette Classics is a newer museum featuring 51 of the finest restored and judged classic Corvettes of the 50's, 60's, 70's, 80's and 90's.

FORT WAYNE KOMETS

Memorial Coliseum

Fort Wayne 46805

❑ Phone: (260) 483-1111, **Web: www.komets.com**

❑ Season: (October-March)

❑ Admission: $8.00-$15.00 adult, $7.00-$12.00 senior (60+), $6.00-$11.00 student (12+), $4.00-$7.00 child.

The longest continual running sports franchise in Fort Wayne. United Hockey League. Look for Icy the mascot.

FORT WAYNE WIZARDS

Memorial Stadium (1616 E. Coliseum Blvd.)

Fort Wayne 46805

❑ Phone: (260) 483-1111 (tickets) or (260) 482-6400 (office) **Web: www.wizardsbaseball.com**

❑ Admission: $6.50-$9.00

This professional baseball team is the Class-A affiliate of the San Diego Padres in the Midwest Baseball League. Look for Dinger the Dragon mascot. Season: April-September.

SCIENCE CENTRAL

1950 North Clinton Street (between State and Fourth Sts.)

Fort Wayne 46805

❑ Phone: (260) 424-2400 or (800) 442-6376 **Web: www.sciencecentral.org**

❑ Hours: Tuesday-Saturday 9:00am-5:00pm, Sunday Noon-5:00 pm.

❑ Admission: $5.50 adult, $5.00 senior (65+), $4.50 child (3-12)

❑ Miscellaneous: Free Parking. The LaboraSTOREy -- A Store for Science offers merchandise that is fun, educational, affordable and unique!

The science/physics playground is housed in the former electric plant. Kids can bend rainbows, create tornadoes and earthquakes, hold a starfish, walk like an astronaut over a moonscape where you weigh next to nothing. Here's a breakdown of the exhibit areas:

- ❑ KIDS CENTRAL - A special area just for kids age 2 through 7 and their grown-ups. Young scientists enter Kids Central through a specially-sized doorway and quickly discover more than 20 hands-on exhibits including a puppet theater, a captured shadow room that lets you play with your shadow like Peter Pan, a giant bubble machine that allows you to actually be inside a bubble, a water table and Fort Discovery - a multi-level play structure.

- ❑ SWAP SHOP - Kids are encouraged to bring in their treasures from nature and trade them with other objects in the Swap Shop collection. Trading is based on a point system and points can be spent or banked for future use.

- ❑ MEASUREMENT GALLERY - Step into a device that checks your horizontal and vertical body measurements. Or step onto a platform that tells you how many gallons of water are in your body. You can even step under a wave field that will give you your exact height. For the athletically inclined, there's a treadmill that will tell you how many calories and BTU's you're expending.

- ❑ OBSERVATION GALLERY - Examine starfish, hermit crabs and other Atlantic Ocean creatures in the Ocean Tidal Pool. Whisper Dishes let you speak into a big parabolic dish to see if your partner can hear you several feet away. Clap into the Echo Tube, launch a wind missile with the Air Cannon, play the piano with your feet, build a self-supporting arch and explore the electrical properties of the human heart.

- ❑ INVESTIGATION GALLERY - Can you lift yourself into the air using ropes and pulleys? Lift yourself with various block and tackle combinations. Build a model structure and see what it takes to destroy it. Drop payloads via parachute.

FORT WAYNE PHILHARMONIC
2340 Fairfield Avenue
Fort Wayne 46807

❑   Phone: (260) 456-2224, **Web: www.fortwaynephilharmonic.com**
❑   Admission: At any Philharmonic Masterworks, Chamber, Stained
      Glass or Freimann Series performance, children grades K-12 may
      attend at no charge with a paid adult admission.

Philharmonic Children's Concerts are presented twice a year in the
Embassy Centre and are designed for children of all ages.
Presented cooperatively with FAME, these concerts are free of
charge. Concert Kids Club is appropriate for Preschool and
Elementary children ages 3-7 years who can participate in hands-
on art and music activities while their families attend Philharmonic
Stained Glass Concerts. Cost is $6.00.

DIEHM WILDLIFE MUSEUM OF NATURAL HISTORY
600 Franke Park Drive
Fort Wayne 46808

❑   Phone: (260) 427-6708
❑   Hours: Wednesday-Sunday Noon-5:00pm (Late April to mid-
      October)
❑   Admission: Small (ages 2+)

North American wildlife mounted in natural settings. There are
written and audio descriptions of each exhibit. Also, see displays
of minerals and gems.

FORT WAYNE CHILDREN'S ZOO

3411 Sherman Blvd (I-69 to Exit 109A - US 33 South)

Fort Wayne 46808

- ❑ Phone: (260) 427-6800, **Web: www.kidszoo.com**
- ❑ Hours: Daily 9:00am-5:00pm. (late April to mid-October)
- ❑ Admission: $6.50 adult, $4.00 senior (60+) and child (2-14). $1-$2.00 rides.
- ❑ Miscellaneous: Lakeside Gazebo. Endangered Species Carousel, Train Ride, Pony Ride, Safari Ride, Boat Ride (additional fee). Tree Tops Cafe.

This zoo really understands kids and their need to have activity and interaction associated with their learning (i.e.. wonderful rides are offered in most areas to enhance the "lifestyle" experience of the land the animal comes from). One of the top children's zoos in the U.S. is highlighted by:

- ❑ INDONESIAN RAIN FOREST - Apes, bats, komodo dragon and giant walking sticks.
- ❑ AFRICAN VELDT - Safari jeep ride on 22 acres of grassland where animals roam free. African village.
- ❑ AUSTRALIAN ADVENTURE - Meet a wallaby and her Joey. Great Barrier Reef tropical fish in 20,000 gallon aquarium. Australia After Dark fruit bats. Matilda's Fish and Chips. Herbst River Ride dugout canoe tour. Tasmanian devils. Kangaroos. Parakeets.
- ❑ CHILDREN'S ZOO - Contact/petting area. Pony rides. 1860 train ride. Penguins, pandas.

FIREFIGHTERS' MUSEUM AND CAFÉ

226 West Washington Blvd.

Fort Wayne 46852

❑   Phone: (260) 426-0051, **Web: www.jimcat.com/local/jcfire.html**
❑   Hours: Monday-Friday 11:00am-2:00pm
❑   Admission: Museum is FREE. Café serves lunch.
❑   Miscellaneous: Just above the Firefighter's Museum is a Cafe where you are surrounded by antique fire engines and firemen's uniforms and tools.

Try a "Life Net" or "Hook and Ladder" sandwich all set in Fort Wayne's old Engine House #3 building. The museum showcases artifacts used by some of the city's earliest heroes - the firefighters. It has preserved the history of the Fort Wayne Fire Department and also gives tours (by appointment) to teach fire safety. Dine among the artifacts in the Café! Say "Hi" to the Dalmatian for us.

AMISHVILLE USA

844 East 900 South (1-69 to Highway 218 to US 27 - Follow signs from Berne)

Geneva 46740

❑   Phone: (260) 589-3536, **Web: www.amishville.com**
❑   Hours: Monday-Saturday 9:00am-5:00pm.
     Sunday 11:00am-5:00 pm. (April – December)
❑   Admission: Varies with activity.
❑   Tours: Of Amish Home: $2.75 adult, $1.50 child (6-12).
❑   Miscellaneous: Gift Shop. Essen Platz (eating place) - Amish & Swiss recipes and Country Harvest Buffet (moderate pricing). Working Gristmill on premises (can even buy product). Buggy rides of farm area, $1.25/person (ages 3+). Campsites on property available.

The tour of an Old Order Amish Home was the highlight of this visit. The guide includes the children in descriptions of a typical day - for instance, Sally would go fetch eggs while Johnny would milk cows or feed horses. A little girl or boy is chosen from the tour to be the "model" as they are adorned with different clothes to match their age (i.e. a young girl always wears her hair in two braids with no bangs with a bonnet and dress). Pins and occasional buttons are used in clothing - never shiny zippers. Young brides only change their outer apron for the wedding. See how families survive without electricity or plumbing and how close the families are (grandparents live in a house next to the main house). Set back on a country road lined with traditional Amish farms and buggies as people go about their daily chores. Truly authentic "Amishcana"!

LIMBERLOST STATE HISTORIC SITE

200 East 6th Street (one block east of US 27)

Geneva 46740

- ❑   Phone: (260) 368-7428, **Web: www.ai.org/ism/sites/limberlost**
- ❑   Hours: Wednesday-Saturday 9:00am-5:00pm, Sunday 1:00-5:00pm (last tour at 4:30pm). Closed Thanksgiving, Christmastime, New Years and Easter. Closed mid-December to mid-March.
- ❑   Admission: FREE, donations accepted.

Stretching for 13 thousand acres across the vast forest and swampland was a legend for its quicksand and unsavory characters. The swamp received its name from the fate of Limber Jim Corbus, who went hunting in the swamp and never returned. When the locals asked where Jim Corbus was, the familiar cry was "Limber's lost!" To Gene Stratton-Porter, the swamp was her playground, laboratory and inspiration. The swamp was the subject of her acclaimed books and photographs.

HOME OF ELIAS RUFF RESTAURANT

Main Street (Behind Antiques Shopping Complex)

Grabill 46741

❑   Phone: (260) 627-6312

❑   Hours: Daily 11:00am-8:00pm

Pretend you're a traveling pioneer family for a day and stop at the 200 year old reconstructed roadhouse. All furnishings are period 1800's including the "pie safe", the oil lamps at each table, and the large cupboard that opens up to serve from the kitchen. While it is suggested one-person order the Blue Plate Special (old country recipes served on a speckled blue tin plate), you're safe with any dish (all are plainly seasoned).

GREENFIELD MILLS

1050 East 7560 North

Howe 46746

❑   Phone: (260) 367-2394

❑   Hours: Monday-Friday 7:00am-5:00pm

❑   Tours: By appointment only. Fee for tours is $0.50-$2.00.

A family-owned working mill since 1846. Hydroelectric generators now provide power to mill soft wheat flour.

DAN QUAYLE CENTER AND MUSEUM

815 Warren Street (I-69 at US 224 or US 24 exit - Downtown corner of Warren and Tipton Streets)

Huntington 46750

❑   Phone: (260) 356-6356, **Web: www.quaylemuseum.org**

❑   Hours: Tuesday-Saturday 10:00am-4:00pm, Sunday 1:00-4:00pm. Closed major holidays.

❑   Admission: Suggested donations $3.00 adult, $1.50 child

Dan Quayle Center (cont.)

❑   Miscellaneous: Large screen video presentation. Gift Shop.

America's only Vice-Presidential museum specifically dedicated to J. Danforth Quayle, 44th Vice-President. Trace Quayle's early years growing up in Huntington along with his political career. See his report card from local schools and pictures with Presidents. Exhibits and educational programs focus on the history and politics behind our nation's Vice-Presidents with spotlights on the five Vice-Presidents from Indiana.

FORKS OF THE WABASH HISTORIC PARK

3010 West Park Drive (U524 and SR 9)

Huntington 46750

❑   Phone: (260) 356-1903, **Web: www.historicforks.org**
❑   Hours: Saturday-Sunday 1:00-5:00pm (May-September)
❑   Admission: $1.00-$2.00

After stopping in the Visitor's Center, start your visit of the museum and historical park that tells the story of the relationship between early European settlers and the Miami Indians (lots of trading) and the US Government (treaties). The park includes a log schoolhouse, Nuck family pioneer house of German farmers and most interestingly, the home of Miami Chief Richardville. The chief was considered a skilled negotiator in treaty talks and the wealthiest Native American in North America at his death.

HUNTINGTON LAKE STATE RESERVOIR

517 North Warren Road (off Rte. 5)

Huntington 46750

❑   Phone: (260) 468-2165
      Web: www.in.gov/dnr/parklake/reservoirs/huntington.html
❑   Admission: $3.00-$5.00 per vehicle

J. Edward Roush Lake. Archery Range, Basketball Courts, Mountain Bike Trail, Horseshoes & Croquet, Model Airport, Volleyball Courts on beach.

PIZZA JUNCTION
201 Court Street
Huntington 46750

❑   Phone: (260) 356-4700
❑   Hours: Sunday-Thursday 11:00am-11:00pm. Friday-Saturday
       11:00am-1:00am.

Located by the railroad tracks in a restored train depot. It's really fun when a train goes past. Actual restored photos of historic buildings around town (like Nick's Kitchen) and the original freight depot. Warm weather dining outside by the tracks. Their subs and soup are great too.

WINGS OF FREEDOM MUSEUM
1365 Warren Road (Huntington Municipal Airport - I-69 to SR 5)
Huntington 46750

❑   Phone: (260) 356-1945
❑   Hours: Saturday 10:00am-4:00pm, Sunday 1:00-4:00pm (May-
       October)
❑   Admission: $2.00 adult, $1.00 child (age 6+)

The museum was created to preserve the legacy of pilots and their support crews who faced war to secure American freedoms. The central focus is a P-51D Mustang flown in successful combats by World War II fighter ace pilot, Brigadier General Robin Olds. The P-51 is flown regularly along with an AT-6. There are also photos, clothing, cockpit instruments and artifacts tracing the history of military aviation.

INDIANA HISTORIC RADIO MUSEUM
800 Lincolnway South
Ligonier 46767

❑   Phone: (260) 894-9000
❑   Hours: Tuesday, Wednesday, Thursday and Saturday 10:00am-
     3:00pm (May-October). Saturday only 10:00am-2:00pm
     (Winter).
❑   Admission: FREE

Tour Indiana's only radio museum featuring over 400 antique
radios. Visitors Bureau offers pre-arranged tours of homes,
museums and gardens.

GENE STRATTON PORTER STATE HISTORIC SITE
1205 Pleasant Point (5 miles west of Kendallville on US 6 and 3
miles north on SR 9)
Rome City 46784

❑   Phone: (260) 854-3790, **Web: www.ai.org/ism/sites/porter**
❑   Hours: Tuesday-Saturday 9:00am-5:00pm, Sunday 1:00-5:00pm.
     Closed Thanksgiving, Christmastime, New Years and Easter.
     Closed mid-December to mid-March.
❑   Admission: FREE, donations accepted.
❑   Tours: Guided Cabin Tours given on the hour. Last tour at
     4:00pm.
❑   Miscellaneous: Picnic facilities, lakefront accessibility, hiking
     trails.

"The Cabin in the Wildflower Woods" lies nestled on the shore of
Sylvan Lake, near Rome City, Indiana. It is the second Indiana
home of Hoosier author, naturalist, photographer, Gene Stratton
Porter. Furnishings in the home are arranged and maintained to
reflect -- as authentically as possible -- the Porter's lifestyle. Much
of the furniture and personal memorabilia, including Mrs. Porter's

library, are preserved at the home. In her lifetime, 1863-1924, Porter authored 12 novels, seven nature books, two books of poetry, children's books and numerous magazine articles. Eight of her novels were produced as motion pictures.

BUGGY LINE TOURS

(SR 5, across from flea market)

Shipshewana 46565

- ❑ Phone: (888) 44BUGGY, **Web: www.buggylinetours.com**
- ❑ Admission: $5.00 per person (ride only). $8.00 30 minute tour. $14.00-$15.00 one hour tour. Children 4 and under FREE.
- ❑ Tours: Tuesday, Wednesday, Friday and Saturday. Seasonally. Thresher meal at Amish Home Tuesday & Wednesday Buggy rides (30 min.- One Hour) between 10:00am-4:30pm.

Buggy rides, backroads country tours (in 15 passenger air-conditioned van), step-on guides and Amish farm tours. 1 - 3 Hour Sight-Seeing Tours or 15 minute rides thru town.

MENNO-HOF, MENNONITE-AMISH VISITORS CENTER

510 South Van Buren Street (North of US 20 and SR 5)

Shipshewana 46565

- ❑ Phone: (260) 768-4117
- ❑ Hours: Monday-Saturday, 10:00am-5:00pm. (Adjusted seasonally, especially Winter)
- ❑ Admission: Donation. Suggested - Adults $4.00, Children $2.00
- ❑ Tours: One hour
- ❑ Miscellaneous: Most of the tour is "over the heads" of children twelve years and under; however, you can advise your guide of this and they can accommodate by spending significant time in the Interactive Room.

Where can you take one journey starting in a courtyard in 1525, in Europe, around a water pitcher? Then, get locked in a dungeon, escape in a cramped quarters ship, survive a tornado and learn about the power of faith! About halfway through, children will have the chance to walk around and play in an Amish built (beams, pegs and kneebraces only) barn stocked with simple wood toys. Our kids had to be pulled away - we may never buy "gadget" toys again! This is a very thorough walking tour of the story of tragedy and triumph of a people searching for peace. Afterwards, you'll truly understand the reasons for their way of life.

SECHLER'S FINE PICKLES

5686 SR 1 (1-69 North to DuPont Exit to SR 1 North - 20 miles)

St. Joe 46785

- ❑   Phone: (260) 337-5461or (800)332-5461
     Web: www.gourmetpickles.com
- ❑   Admission: FREE
- ❑   Viewing Times: Monday-Friday 9:00-11:00 am & 1:00-3:00 pm.;
     Saturday 8:30am-Noon (April-October). Showroom open
     weekdays until 4:30pm.
- ❑   Miscellaneous: Retail showroom has sample table with one of
     each variety pickle available to taste. Try flavors like jalapeno
     slices, orange or candied raisin crispies.

Pucker up for pickles! Ralph Sechler began pickle processing in 1921 in his home (next to the factory). Pickles are just cucumbers, salt, water, vinegar and spices but the secret combination prepares just the right taste. Around the side of the building, you might see truckloads of "cukes" arrive (farmers are paid the highest price for "gherkins", the smallest) and sorted into slots for seven different sizes. Each size is processed in covered vats full of salt brine for 2½ months to 1½ years depending upon demand. Before pickles are packaged, they are first cooked for 24 hours, then sliced, chopped or ground and left to marinate 1-10 days in special spice solutions. Workers stand by special stainless steel tables and hand-pack each variety in its special brine. Our favorite flavor is sweet apple cinnamon. Be sure to take some of the 40 varieties home!

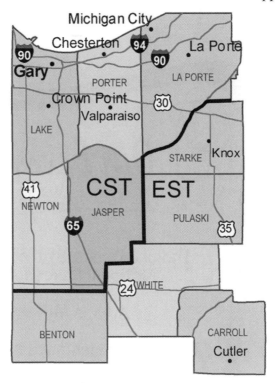

Chapter 6
North West Area

Our Favorites...

Indiana Dunes State Park & National Lakeshore

Adams Mill

Twinrocker Handmade Paper

Waterparks

TWINROCKER HANDMADE PAPER

100 East Third Street (downtown, by railroad tracks)

Brookston 47923

- ❑   Phone: (765) 563-3119 or (800) 757-TWIN
  Web: www.dcwi.com/~twinrock
- ❑   Hours: Monday-Friday 9:00am-3:00pm
- ❑   Admission: $4.00/person (1-10 people), $3.00/person (11+ people in group).
- ❑   Tours: By appointment. Ages 8+. Open tours at 1:30 pm Tuesdays.
- ❑   Miscellaneous: All handmade papers are discounted 25% for the tour group. ("Seconds" are discounted 30 to 50%).

The painstaking, lost art of making sheet paper by hand is back and Twinrocker was among the first hand mills to open in the 70's. Watch "cooked" cotton, husk or linen rag fibers turn into custom paper. Individuals, families, and small and large groups up to 70 are welcome to visit Twinrocker to take a tour of the paper studio. A Twinrocker staff member will speak to your group about the history and practice of this ancient craft while you watch them at work. A tour is 30 to 40 minutes. Visitors are welcome to see the large selection of papers for watercolor, pastel, calligraphy, printmaking, drawing and stationery. You'll see them first beat the fiber with water which we learned releases cellulose causing fiber and water to bond. Next a mould or sieve is dipped into the vat of pulp and shaken. The new sheet formed is "couched" between pieces of wool felt, pressed and then dried. As the paper dries and water evaporates, the fibers bond closer. A special copywritten exaggerated "Feather" deckle edge is the company signature.

INDIANA DUNES STATE PARK / NATIONAL LAKESHORE

1600 N 25 E (3 miles East of SR 49, Kemil Road at US 12)

Chesterton 46304

- ❑   Phone: (219) 926-1952
     Web: www.in.gov/dnr/parklake/parks/indianadunes.html
- ❑   Hours: Dawn to dusk.
- ❑   Admission: $3.00-$5.00 per vehicle.
- ❑   Miscellaneous: Offers swimming, hiking, beach house, concessions, camping, playground equipment and picnic shelters. Nature center has year-round program for all ages

The Nature Center offers a 12 minute video about dunes and surrounding plant life that is helpful to watch before exploring. The largest "live" dune, Mt. Baldy ("live" means it still moves as wind lifts grains of sand & drops them) is guaranteed to make your mouth drop and your eyes open wide. It's a thrill to climb quickly to the top (123 ft.) and let the dune slide you down to the water's edge. (Note to Parents: be ready for an aerobic workout!). On a windy day, place a beach toy on the sand and watch a mini-dune form behind it! On a windy day you can also hear the sand "sing" under your feet – it's true! Swimming/Beach. Another site to visit (esp. during special events) is the Bailly Homestead and Chellberg Farm. Visit the home of one of Porter County's earliest settlers, French-Canadian voyageur and fur trader Joseph Bailly. Nearby is an early 20th century 80-acre working farm established in 1874 by Swedish immigrants Anders and Johanna Kjellberg, who emigrated from Sweden in 1863. (Both properties on Mineral Springs Road, between U.S. Highways 12 and 20, Porter. 219-926-7561, extension 225).

DEEP RIVER WATERPARK

9001 E. US 30, (off I-65)

Crown Point 46307

❑   Phone: (800) WAV-PARK or (219) 947-7349
    Web: www.deepriverwaterpark.com
❑   Hours: Daily 10:00am-6:00pm (Memorial Day Weekend - Labor
    Day, excluding the last two Monday-Fridays in August). Central
    Time.
❑   Admission: $14.00 General, Half Price for child (under 46").
❑   Miscellaneous: Park is available for private parties after 6:30PM.

There is a lot to do at this Waterpark including a wave pool, lazy
river, Tube and Body slides, Paddles Playland and many
adventurous waterslides like "The Storm" tunnel tube ride.

ADAMS MILL

(1/2 mile east of town on Rte. 500 south)

Cutler 46920

❑   Phone: (765) 463-7893
❑   Hours: Weekends 1:00-5:00pm (May-October), 11:00am-5:00pm
    for events (usually held once per month).
❑   Admission: $5.00 family, $2.00 adult, $1.00 child.

A grist mill with hundreds of pioneer life antiques displayed. A
display of "Americana". Most of the original mill equipment is
running. Monthly ground events are the best time to visit.

JOHN DILLINGER MUSEUM

7770 Corrinne Drive (I-90/90 at Kennedy Ave. South, right at first
light - Visitors Center)

Hammond 46323

❑   Phone: (219) 989-7979, **Web: www.johndillingermuseum.com**

John Dillinger Museum (cont.)

❑ Hours: Monday-Friday 8:00am-5:00pm, Saturday-Sunday
9:00am-5:00pm.

❑ Admission: $4.00 adult, $3.00 child or senior.

An interactive museum depicting the Dillinger era with wax
figures and original "tools" used to escape prison.

WOOD'S HISTORIC GRIST MILL

9410 Old Lincoln Highway (in Deep River County Park)

Hobart 46342

❑ Phone: (219) 769-9030 or (219) 947-1958
Web: www.netnitco.net/deepriver/deepriver.html

❑ Hours: Daily 10:00am-5:00pm (May-October)

❑ Admission: FREE (child 12 and under). $0.50 adult.

❑ Miscellaneous: General Store - old fashioned wooden floors, jars
of candy and sundries.

Restored late 1800's mill designed to expose you to the process of
a gristmill and pioneer life. The first floor is where the raw grain is
ground by large stones. The other two floors are displays of period
settings. Also take a peek in the 1830's sawmill.

STARKE COUNTY HISTORICAL MUSEUM

401 S. Main Street (2 blocks west of US 35)

Knox 46534

❑ Phone: (574) 772-5393

❑ Hours: Tuesday-Friday Noon-4:00pm.

❑ Admission: FREE

❑ Miscellaneous: Annual events include the July 4th Ice Cream
Social and a Christmas Open House.

Starke County Historical Museum is quartered in the home of
banker, businessman, twice-elected Governor of Indiana, Henry F.

Schricker. The museum holds three floors of historical memorabilia including agricultural, military items, clothing, decorative items, toys, a schoolroom and the Schricker Room containing the family's personal collections. Take a guided tour of the house.

BASS LAKE STATE BEACH

5838 SR 10

Knox 47534

❑ Phone: (574) 772-3382 Summer and (219) 946-3213 Winter
   Web: www.in.gov/dnr/parklake/parks/basslake.html
❑ Admission: $3.00-$5.00 per vehicle.

Located in northwest Indiana, Bass Lake is Indiana's fourth largest natural lake. Swimming and wading are offered, with shaded areas on portions of the swimming beach. A bathhouse provides showers, changing rooms and vending machines. Unlimited power boating is available too.

DOOR PRAIRIE AUTO MUSEUM

2405 Indiana Avenue (1 mile south of town on US 35)

LaPorte 46350

❑ Phone: (219) 326-1337, **Web: www.dpautomuseum.com**
❑ Hours: Tuesday-Saturday 10:00am-4:30pm, Sunday Noon-
   4:30pm (April-December 23). Central Time.
❑ Admission: $5.00 adult, $4.00 senior (60+), $3.00 youth (10-18).

The collection covers 100 years - beginning with an example of the world's first car, an 1886 Benz Motor Wagon. There are also Auburn, Bricklin, Citroen, Daimler, Duesenberg, Duryea, Ford, Mercedes, Mitchell, Rolls Royce, Studebaker, Tucker, Winton and many others. The Indiana Room shows a complete set of license plates from 1913 to the present. Also featured are antique toys, historic airplanes, and a walk down main street featuring business store fronts from the 1900's, 1940's and 1960's. Self-guided.

LAPORTE COUNTY MUSEUM

809 State Street (State and Michigan Avenue)

LaPorte 46350

- ❑ Phone: (219) 326-6808, **Web: www.lapcohistsoc.org**
- ❑ Hours: Tuesday-Saturday 10:00am-4:30pm
- ❑ Admission: FREE

With over 80,000 items on display, this museum houses LaPorte County family heirlooms and the W. A. Jones collection of antique firearms and weapons.

ABC CHILDREN'S MUSEUM

2921 Franklin Street

Michigan City 46360

- ❑ Phone: (219) 874-8222
- ❑ Hours: Tuesday-Friday Noon-5:00pm, Saturday 10:00am-5:00pm.
- ❑ Admission: $3.50 adult, $2.50 student.
- ❑ Tours: By appointment (weekdays)

This Tudor home has 12 exhibit areas. Hands-on, interactive exhibits explore science principles, nature, sounds, music, color, light and culture. Children ages 3 to 10 will enjoy the new "Discovery Town" theme. Explore the travel agency, town factory, fossil dig, puppet treehouse and more.

ACTING THEATRE OF MICHIGAN CITY

215 West 10th Street

Michigan City 46360

- ❑ Phone: (219) 872-4221

Indiana's only all-original theatre. Productions year-round featuring dance, music, lights, comedy and drama for the family in a unique 75-seat theatre. Workshops for children.

GREAT LAKES MUSEUM OF MILITARY HISTORY

360 Dunes Plaza, US 20

Michigan City 46360

❑   Phone: (219) 872-2702
      Web: www.militaryhistorymuseum.org
❑   Hours: Tuesday-Friday 9:00am-4:00pm, Saturday 10:00am-
      4:00pm, Sunday (Summer) Noon-4:00pm. Closed Thanksgiving,
      Christmastime and New Years.
❑   Admission: $2.00 adult, $1.00 senior and youth (9-18)
❑   Miscellaneous: Displays of memorabilia from all eras includes
      photos, weapons, medals, uniforms, World War II Declarations
      of War, and a 1905 Cannon. The first submarine was launched
      from these shores.

HESSTON STEAM MUSEUM

313 Kintzele Road (2.5 miles east of SR 39 on County. Rd. 1000N)

Michigan City 46360

❑   Phone: (219) 778-2783 or (219) 872-7405
      Web: www.hesston.org
❑   Hours: Weekends Noon-5:00pm (Memorial Day-Labor Day).
      Sunday only (September-October).
❑   Admission: FREE, except on Labor Day weekend.

Three gauges of steam trains give rides around 155 wooded acres,
climbing a grade, crossing several dams, running alongside ponds
or dams and depots. Also, steam crane, sawmill, traction engine
and threshing machines, power plant and more.

OLD LIGHTHOUSE MUSEUM

Heisman Harbor Road

Michigan City 46360

- ❑ Phone: (219) 872-6133
- ❑ Hours: Daily 1:00-4:00pm (except Monday). Closed January and February.
- ❑ Admission: $2.00 general, $0.50 child (12 and younger)

An original 1858 lighthouse filled with displays of recreated keeper's house, lake lore, ship wrecks, and maritime history. Take the cat walk out to the only operational lighthouse in Indiana. Learn how the lighthouse keeper and his/her family (the most famous keeper was a woman) lived and worked.

WASHINGTON PARK ZOO

115 Lake Shore Drive

Michigan City 46360

- ❑ Phone: (219) 873-1510
  Web: www.emichigancity.com/cityhall/departments/zoo/
- ❑ Hours: Daily, mostly afternoons (April-December). Call first as hours are seasonally changing and are open most for tours and events.
- ❑ Admission: $2.00-$3.00

A 1928 zoo laid out on the side of a wooded sand dune. One of the oldest and largest zoos with a petting area (near the entrance), children's castle, feline house, turtle pond, bobcat/prairie dog display and monkey island. You also can see the Michigan shoreline and Chicago skyline from the observation tower.

INDIANA BEACH AMUSEMENT

5224 East Indiana Beach Road (I-65 to US 24)

Monticello 47960

❑   Phone: (574) 583-4141, **Web: www.indianabeach.com**
❑   Hours: Summer hours 11:00am-11:00pm. (mid May-Labor Day)
❑   Admission: $3.00 general (age 4+) plus Ride Plans $10.00 -
     $15.00 (or $1.00-2.00 per ride). Waterpark passes are additional
     $13.00.
❑   Miscellaneous: Camp Resort. Free Parking.

The 1400 acre lake with sandy beach provides a day full of
entertainment without an excessive entrance fee. Popular
amusements are the "Den of Lost Thieves" and "Hoosier
Hurricane" or "Corn Ball Express" rides along with Kiddieland,
an arcade, mini-golf, and mini-train rides. Browse or eat at the
Boardwalk and then watch a Water Ski show after you've taken
the plunge on the "Big Flush" waterslide in the WaterPark. To
relax, try a ride on the "Shafer Queen" paddle wheel boat or watch
a live entertainment show.

SPLASH DOWN DUNES WATER PARK

150 East US 20 (1 mile South of The Indiana Dunes State Park)

Porter 46304

❑   Phone: (219) 929-1181, **Web: www.splashdowndunes.com**
❑   Hours: Daily 10:00am-8:00pm (Summer). Open till 6:00pm
     (mid-August until Labor Day).
❑   Admission:$10 - $15.00 range. Children 3 and under free.
❑   Miscellaneous: Gift shop and arcade. Concessions.

Giant Twister is a series of 11 slides all twisting by each other;
The Tower – Indiana's tallest slide is 68'; Big Wave is the
Midwest's largest wave pool; a lazy river; and Sandcastle Bay -
Kids "hang out" for little ones under 4 feet tall including shorter,
wider slides.

HOOSIER BAT COMPANY

4511 East Evans Avenue (SR 49 bypass exit Hwy. 2 east, left at railroad tracks)

Valparaiso 46383

- ❑ Phone: (800) 228-3787
- ❑ Admission: FREE
- ❑ Tours: Mornings best. Advance notice. Ages 8+. 45 minutes to one hour long. Max. 20 people.

Created by a former scout for the New York Yankees, Hoosier Bats are making an appearance on the major league scene. Chicago Cub Sammy Sosa used one to break his slump in 1998 and become National League MVP. Each year, more than 30,000 custom bats are manufactured for teams such as the White Sox, Mariners, Orioles, Indians and Brewers. Watch the patented, three-piece wood bats being made, then buy your own Hoosier Bat (or, just purchase a smaller souvenir bat in their gift shop).

PORTER COUNTY OLD JAIL MUSEUM

152 South Franklin Street

Valparaiso 46383

- ❑ Phone: (219) 465-3595
- ❑ Hours: Saturday, Sunday, Wednesday 1:00-4:00pm
- ❑ Admission: FREE

The Sheriff's home is an Italianate brick building that contains rooms of period furniture. The jail is a two-story structure leading to the Sheriff's home. See WWII pectoral marquetry artwork, an exhibit on Wild West Bronco John (Buffalo Bill's partner) and dress from the Inaugural Ball of Abe Lincoln.

GUSE CHRISTMAS TREE FARM

6177 West 1450 South

Wanatah 46390

❑ Phone: (219) 733-9346
❑ Hours: Daily 8:00am-4:00pm (Thanksgiving-Christmas Eve).
❑ Admission: FREE
❑ Tours: By appointment. 45 minutes long. (mid-November to mid-December)

This is a 3rd and 4th generation year round business raising Christmas trees. 125 acres of trees show how different trees grow, how Christmas wreaths are made, and the operations it takes to make the finest trees. Come and cut or dig a Douglas, Fraiser Fir, Scotch, White Pine or Blue Spruce. Enjoy horse-drawn carriage rides every weekend. Warm up with hot cocoa.

TIPPECANOE RIVER STATE PARK

4200 North US 35

Winamac 46996

❑ Phone: (574) 946-3213, **Web:**
   www.in.gov/dnr/parklake/parks/tippecanoeriver.html
❑ Admission: $3.00-$5.00 per vehicle.

This park is most used for the bridle trails and excellent canoeing. During the summer when you want to swim, just take your current gate or campground receipt to Bass Lake State Beach for free admission. Warning: mosquitoes can be very annoying at times during the season. Repellent is advised! Also camping, hiking, fishing and seasonal programs (like cross-country skiing in winter).

Chapter 7

South East Area

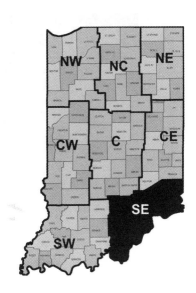

130

Our Favorites...

Forest Discovery Center

Squire Boone Caverns & Village

Zimmerman Art Glass

Falls of the Ohio

DEAM LAKE STATE FOREST

1217 Deam Lake Road, SR 60

Borden 47106

❑   Phone: (812) 246-5421

Web: www.state.in.us/dnr/forestry/property/deamlake.htm

Named for Indiana's first state forester, this area has camping, fishing, boating, swimming, rowboat rentals, hiking trails and a Nature Center.

BROWNSTOWN SPEEDWAY

Hwy. 250, one mile southeast of town (Jackson County Fairgrounds)

Brownstown 47220

❑   Phone: (812) 358-5332, **Web: www.brownstownspeedway.com**
❑   Hours: Racing Saturdays at 7:00pm (March-October).

Stock car races including Late Models, Modifieds, Street Stocks, and Bombers. Admission charged.

JACKSON-WASHINGTON STATE FOREST

1278 East SR 250

Brownstown 47220

❑   Phone: (812) 358-2160

Web: www.state.in.us/dnr/forestry/property/jackson.htm

Skyline View, Archery Range, Basketball and Volleyball Courts, Bridle Trails.

CHARLESTOWN STATE PARK

PO Box 38 (west of SR 62)

Charlestown 47111

❑ Phone: (812) 256-5600
Web: www.in.gov/dnr/parklake/parks/charlestown.html
❑ Hours: Open year-round.
❑ Admission: $3.00/vehicle (in-state), $5.00/vehicle (out-of-state).

Devonian fossils, Bird Watchers, Hiking (rugged and moderate trails available); Formerly part of the Indiana Ammunition Plant - so much of the ground is unspoiled; Camping area on site.

DERBY DINNER PLAYHOUSE

525 Marriott Drive

Clarksville 47129

❑ Phone: (812) 288-2632 or (812) 288-8281 tickets
Web: www.derbydinner.com
❑ Hours: Performances Tuesday - Sunday
❑ Doors open at 6:00pm for Buffet Dinner - Show starts at 8:00pm
❑ Matinees - Wednesday & Sunday
❑ Doors open at 11:45am - Show at 1:30pm
❑ Tickets: $25.00-$37.00. Senior Citizen's and Children's Discount on Friday and Sunday Evenings.

A dinner theater in the round featuring top-notch performances of Broadway productions served after a buffet dinner. Shows run for approximately 6 weeks and special shows are offered periodically. Children's theatre programs offered of seasonal themes or cartoon favorites (breakfast and lunch shows for these performances).

FALLS OF THE OHIO STATE PARK

201 West Riverside Drive (I – 65 Exit 0, follow signs)

Clarksville 47129

- ❑ Phone: (812) 280-9970, **Web: www.fallsoftheohio.org**
- ❑ Hours: Center open Monday-Saturday 9:00am-5:00pm, Sunday 1:00-5:00pm. Park open daily dawn to dusk. Closed Thanksgiving and Christmas
- ❑ Admission: $4.00 adult, $1.00 child (under age 19).
- ❑ Tours: Guided tours of fossil beds May-October (EDST). Classrooms November-April.
- ❑ Miscellaneous: Boat Launch Ramp/Ohio River, Hiking Trails, Picnicking, Bird Watching, Fishing, Gift Shop, and
- ❑ Ohio River and Coral Reef Aquariums.

The "Age of Fish" coral reef fossil beds are among the largest exposed Devonian fossil beds in the world. The park features a spectacular visitor center overlooking the fossil beds containing an exhibit and video presentation. While fossil collecting is prohibited, visitors are free to explore – we could identify corals, sponges, sea shells and snails. The months of August through October are the most accessible as the river is at its lowest level. Tip: It was suggested to splash water on a colony area and they will "jump out" showing exquisite detail. The Interpretive Center features a full size mammoth skeleton, plus there are exhibits on geology, history and cultural development of the Falls of the Ohio.

CORYDON CAPITOL STATE HISTORIC SITE

202 East Walnut Street (I-64 exit 105 to downtown)

Corydon 47112

- ❑ Phone: (812) 738-4890, **Web: www.ai.org/ism/sites/corydon**
- ❑ Hours: Tuesday-Saturday 9:00am-5:00pm, Sunday 1:00-5:00pm. Closed Thanksgiving, Christmas Eve, Christmas Day, New Year's Day and Easter. Closed mid-December to mid-March.
- ❑ Admission: FREE. Donations accepted.

Corydon Capitol (cont.)

❑   Miscellaneous: Guided tours, visitor center and gift shop. Several
        Special events are also held to celebrate Indiana's heritage.

This Site includes the restored 1816 limestone state capitol
building, Governor's residence, and first state office building
among other landmarks in the area. Limestone was hauled from
nearby quarries to erect the 40 foot square walls, and poplar and
walnut logs were cut from virgin forests from the ceiling and roof
supports. In June of 1816, 43 delegates met in Corydon to draft the
first state constitution. Much of their work was done under the
shade of a huge elm tree. The trunk of the tree, now known as the
"Constitution Elm," is still standing. The State Historic Site
recounts Indiana's early days of statehood.

CORYDON SCENIC RAILROAD

210 W. Walnut (Walnut and Water Streets, one mile south of I-64)

Corydon 47112

❑   Phone: (812) 738-8000
❑   Hours: Wednesday-Sunday (mid-June to mid-August) Weekends
        only (late May-September, October and early November)
❑   Admission: Adults $9.00, Seniors $1.00 off, Children $5.00 (4+).
❑   Tours: 1:00 pm weekdays, 1:00 & 3:00 pm, weekends and
        holidays. 1 ½ hour ride.
❑   Miscellaneous: Group tours 30+. Air-conditioned. Train depot -
        memorabilia and snacks.

All aboard the Silverliner train. The 115 year old railroad passes by
the history of 1820's Corydon on 16 miles of track in the Indiana
countryside. The passenger train is a historic model with large
windows and comfortable seats. Occasional musical entertainment.

HARRISON CRAWFORD STATE FOREST / WYANDOTTE COMPLEX STATE FOREST

7240 Old Forest Road SW (bordering the Ohio River)

Corydon 47112

❑ Phone: (812) 738-8232, **Web: www.cccn.net**

Timber is the key resource consideration in the management and use of Indiana's State Forests. The timber is continually evaluated to determine management needs such as harvesting, planting, thinning or timber stand improvement. Openings created by timber harvesting also increase wildlife habitat. These openings guarantee stable and healthy populations of both game and non-game species. Recreation here includes fishing, canoeing, a campground, an Olympic size swimming pool, a forestry interpretive center, several picnic areas, and hiking and horse trails.

ZIMMERMAN ART GLASS COMPANY

395 Valley Road (I-64 exit 105 to SR 135 South to SR 62 to Mulberry (right turn) to Valley Road- left turn)

Corydon 47112

❑ Phone: (812) 738-2206
❑ Hours: Tuesday-Saturday 9:00am-3:00pm.
❑ Admission: FREE
❑ Tours: 30 minute demos, Tuesday-Friday only 10:00am-1:00pm or 2:00-4:00pm.
❑ Miscellaneous: Recently produced and signed art glass pieces available on site for purchase – you just have to wait until they finish the piece they're working on.

Generations old and world renowned glass artisans make hand-blown glass paperweights, lamps, bowls and bottles. Two brothers work in a small workshop in an authentic workspace so small that you can stand close to the artist. Watch as they get a glob of premixed colored molten glass and, by constantly twirling it on a long stick, begin to use old world tools to shape the "glob" into their signature "flower". After a few cycles of heating/ shaping/cooling the flower, they let it "twirl cool" to make the final paperweight with a blossomed flower inside. You have to see this remarkable process! Our group was speechless and mesmerized to the point that we didn't even ask questions.

CLARK STATE FOREST
PO Box 119
Henryville 47126

❑   Phone: (812) 294-4306
     Web: www.state.in.us/dnr/forestry/property/clark.htm
❑   Miscellaneous: Camping, Hiking Trails, Seven Fishing Lakes, and Bridle Trails.

HOWARD STEAMBOAT MUSEUM
1101 East Market Street (I-65, exit 0)
Jeffersonville 47130

❑   Phone: (812) 283-3728 or (888) 472-0606
     Web: www.steamboatmuseum.org
❑   Hours: Tuesday-Saturday 10:00am-4:00pm, Sunday 1:00-4:00pm. Closed major holidays.
❑   Admission: $5.00 adult, $4.00 senior, $3.00 students (age 6 thru college).

The museum has a large collection of steamboat models, tools, artifacts, etc. from the Great Steamboat Era. The 1894 Victorian Mansion also has many of the original furnishings and family possessions. The mansion was built by the Howard's, premier steamboat builders. Kids love seeing all the stained glass windows, especially when the sun shines through.

SCHIMPFF'S CONFECTIONERY

347 Spring Street

Jeffersonville 47130

❑   Phone: (812) 283-8367, **Web: www.worldexpositioncenter.com**

Famous for their cinnamon red hots. Schimpff's is a fourth generation, family-owned business that features a soda fountain, original tin ceiling, antique memorabilia and tasty candies.

SPORTSDROME SPEEDWAY

(I-65 exit 4, south on East Frontage Rd)

Jeffersonville 47130

❑   Phone: (812) 282-7551
❑   Hours: April-October

1/4 Mile, slightly banked asphalt oval has Saturday night modified, street stocks, and Dromer Figure 8's.

LAWRENCEBURG SPEEDWAY

351 East Eads Parkway (I-275 exit SR 50, Dearborn County Fairgrounds)

Lawrenceburg 47025

❑   Phone: (812) 539-4700, **Web: http://:home.fuse.net/kewendel**
❑   Hours: Gates Open 5:00pm, Practice laps 6:20pm, Racing 7:00pm. (May-September)
❑   Admission: $10.00 adults, $5.00 youth (11-15), FREE child (10 and under). Pit Passes - $20.00. Prices may vary with sanctioned shows/special events.

1/4 Mile High Banked Clay Oval with weekly racing divisions in Non-wing Sprints, Modifieds and Pro Stocks.

PERFECT NORTH SLOPES

19640 SR 1

Lawrenceburg 47025

❑ Phone: (812) 537-3754 or (513) 381-7517
   Web: www.perfectnorth.com
❑ Hours: Weekdays 10:00am-9:30pm, Weekends 9:00am-3:00am
   (December to mid-March).
❑ Admission: Season Passes $100.00 and up.

With 70 acres of tree-lined trails and wide open slopes, they have skiing for all abilities. They offer ski school, night skiing, equipment rental and purchase.

CLIFTY FALLS STATE PARK

1501 Green Road (off SR 62 or 56)

Madison 47250

❑ Phone: (812) 265-4135 Inn or (812) 273-8885 Park
   Web: www.in.gov/dnr/parklake/parks/cliftyfalls.html
❑ Admission: $3.00-$5.00 per vehicle.

The name Clifty Falls paints a beautiful picture in your mind. Winter and spring hiking trails show the falls at their best while the splendor of the creek and canyon offer exciting scenery year-round. In historic Madison, tour the mansion of frontier banker James F.D. Lanier and enjoy the drive along the beautiful Ohio River. Plan a park visit during one of the community's special events such as the Madison Chautauqua art festival or Regatta hydroplane boat race. Clifty Inn has accommodations and a Restaurant. At the Inn is a seasonal Swimming/Pool with waterslide, tennis & other games. Camping and a Nature Center are here too.

JEFFERSON COUNTY MUSEUM AND RAILROAD STATION DEPOT

615 West First Street (and Mill Streets on Ohio River)

Madison 47250

❏ Phone: (812) 265-2335

    Web: www.seidata.com/~jchs/museum.htm

❏ Hours: Monday-Saturday 10:00am-4:30pm, Sunday 1:00-4:00pm. (May-October). Weekdays only. (November-April)

❏ Admission: $3.00 General.

❏ Miscellaneous: Octagonal Railroad Station (history of first Indiana railroad). Stop over to Dr. William Hutchings' Office (on West 3rd) or The Sullivan House (on West 2nd) for more historical county insight. Located in a historic stone house on the grounds of Madison State Hospital, the new Gatehouse Museum features photos, exhibits and artifacts telling the history of the hospital since its opening in 1910; and tracing the changes over the years in the care of mental patients. (Hours: Thursday - Friday - Saturday - closed winters).

The Pioneer exhibit is a re-created stone house, typical of early rural dwellings. In it is a varied collection of early farming and domestic artifacts. The Steamboat exhibit explains the important role the Ohio River has played in the history of the area. The Civil War exhibit chronicles the famous raid of Confederate General John Hunt Morgan through the county, and explores the roles of soldiers in the Civil War. The Victorian Parlor exhibit highlights period furniture, clothing, artwork, and artifacts, all with a local history.

LANIER MANSION STATE HISTORIC SITE

511 West First Street

Madison 47250

❑   Phone: (812) 265-3526, **Web: www.in.gov/ism/sites/lanier**
❑   Hours: Tuesday-Saturday 9:00am-5:00pm, Sunday 1:00-5:00pm
    (mid March to mid-December). Weekends only (mid December
    to mid-March). The site is closed on Easter, Thanksgiving,
    Christmas Eve, Christmas Day and New Year's Day.
❑   Admission: FREE, donations accepted.

On the banks of the Ohio River stands a stately mansion built for
James Franklin Doughty Lanier - a man who, at one time, saved
Indiana from financial ruin. With national expansion booming,
Lanier's talents as a financier brought him great fortune. The Greek
Revival home is especially noted for its staircases.

MUNDT'S CANDIES / JWI CONFECTIONARY

207 West Main Street (I-65, Ohio River Scenic Route)

Madison 47250

❑   Phone: (812) 265-6171
❑   Hours: Tuesday-Saturday 11:00am-5:00pm, Sunday Noon-
    4:00pm. Open weekend evenings seasonally.

This historic candy store and soda fountain serves gourmet
desserts/ lunches throughout the day. "Lunch at Mundt's" is the
place where the famous "fish" candy is made.

SQUIRE BOONE CAVERNS AND VILLAGE

100 Squire Boone Road SW (I – 64 exit 105. Watch for signs - some pretty tricky)

Mauckport 47142

❑   Phone: (502) 425-CAVE or (812) 732-4382
    Web: www.squireboonecaverns.com

For updates visit our website: www.kidslovepublications.com

- ❑ Hours: 10:00am – 5:00pm. (Memorial Day to mid-August). Weekends only until Labor Day. Pre-scheduled the rest of the year between 10:00am – 4:00pm every two hours. Closed Thanksgiving, Christmas Eve, Christmas, New Years, and weekdays in January and February.
- ❑ Admission: $11.00 adult, $10.00 senior, $6.50 child (6-11). $3.00 parking fee per vehicle in summer. Internet coupons.
- ❑ Tours: Last one hour every 30 minutes. Group packages include hayrides and bonfires.
- ❑ Miscellaneous: Boones 1804 working gristmill – bakery, Gem mining (fossils and gems), soap and candlemaking, petting zoo and playground (Summer only). Caverns are a constant 54 degrees year round. A light jacket is suggested.

Explore the same caverns that Squire and Daniel Boone discovered in 1790 as Squire was out searching for his older brother, Daniel who had been captured by hostile Indians. Walk past stalactites, stalagmites, blind and albino crayfish, underground streams and waterfalls, dams, and the foundation stone carved by Squire himself. It's all very quiet. Squire's life was spared when he hid in the caverns from a band of pursuing Indians – he is even buried in his beloved cave. Buy a spelunking explorer hat with light for the kids to use while they tour. Then they have a great souvenir that was actually used at the site.

PA PAW'S FAMILY FARM

15671 Lewis Road (I-275 exit 16 (Rte. 50) west to Aurora to Rte. 350 west)

Moores Hill 47032

- ❑ Phone: (812) 744-5411(farm) or (513) 821-2011
  Web: www.papawsfarm.homestead.com
- ❑ Hours: Spring-Fall, by reservation.
- ❑ Admission: $85.00 minimum per group ($5.50 per person). Weekday tours are 4 hours, weekend tours are 3 hours.

Pa Paw's Family Farm (cont.)

❑   Miscellaneous: Bring a picnic or party - 3 spacious roofed
        shelters, a wooden red barn and small barn are available for
        learning stations and get-togethers.

Papaw's Family Farm has two main functions: Educational and
Recreational. Enjoy a tour of the farm which features a petting zoo,
palomino horses, goats and pigs. Take a walk along the creek and
sit in a Native American woodland hut replica called a "waken"
while you listen to stories about the Shawnee Indians and how they
survived so many years ago. Learn hands-on about farming, and
how to plant/harvest in the demonstration garden. A large pond
(with nearby shelter) invites ecosystem study. There is a smaller
springfed woodlot pond for comparison. Minutes from the barn
finds a meandering stream, a favorite for exploring students who
wish to find a diversity of woodland wildlife.

CARNEGIE CENTER FOR ARTS & HISTORY/FLOYD COUNTY MUSEUM

201 East Spring Street

New Albany 47150

❑   Phone: (812) 944-7336, **Web: http://carnegie.nafcpl.lib.in.us/**
❑   Hours: Tuesday-Saturday 10:00am-5:30pm.
❑   Admission: FREE, donations accepted.
❑   Miscellaneous: Art and history. "The Yenawire Exhibit" - a
        hand-carved animated diorama depicting scenes from early
        Indiana.

The contemporary art gallery and local history museum has
permanent and temporary traveling exhibits. This is the home of
the famous "Yenowine Folk Art Dioramas - a hand-carved
animated diorama depicting scenes from early Indiana.

CULBERTSON MANSION STATE HISTORIC PARK

914 East Main Street (off I-64)

New Albany 47150

❑ Phone: (812) 244-9600, **Web: www.ai.org/ism/sites/culbertson**
❑ Hours: Tuesday-Saturday 9:00am-5:00pm, Sunday 1:00-5:00pm.
Closed on Mondays, Thanksgiving, Christmas Eve, Christmas
Day, New Year's Day and Easter.
❑ Closed mid-December to mid-March.
❑ Admission: FREE, donations accepted.

A Victorian mansion that stands as an impressive tribute to one of Indiana's leading merchants and philanthropists, William Culbertson. The Culbertson Mansion represents the lifestyles of the Victorian fortune-makers as well as the lifestyles of the servant staffs. Visitors may view the grand parlors, dining rooms, bedrooms, kitchen and laundry room of the 25 room mansion.

VINTAGE FIRE ENGINE MUSEUM

402 Mt. Tabor Road

New Albany 47150

❑ Phone: (812) 941-9901

Rated one of the top five collections of vintage fire apparatus and memorabilia in America, this museum features the very first chemical fire engine in the United States. Other items on display include lanterns, fire engine models, chief's trumpets, engine lamps, torches and more. Watch films on old-time firefighting in the 30-seat theater.

OHIO COUNTY HISTORICAL MUSEUM
212 South Walnut Street
Rising Sun 47040

- ❑ Phone: (812) 438-4915
- ❑ Hours: Daily, except Wednesday 11:00am-4:00pm.
- ❑ Admission: Donation $2.50 adult, $2.00 senior, FREE child (under 12).
- ❑ Miscellaneous: Home of "Hoosier Boy" a 1900 racing boat with fastest time between Louisville and Cincinnati. Auto Harp - first coin operated music player.

HARDY LAKE STATE RESERVOIR
4171 East Harrod Road
Scottsburg 47170

- ❑ Phone: (812) 794-3800
  Web: www.in.gov/dnr/parklake/reservoirs/hardy.html

2,178.16 acres and a 741-acre lake provide facilities like: Archery Range, Sport Courts, Horseshoe Pits, Boating, Camping, Cultural Arts Programs, Fishing / Ice Fishing, Hiking Trails, Interpretive / Recreational Programs, Picnicking /Shelter houses, Playgrounds, Rental-Rowboat, Swimming / Beach, and Water-skiing.

PIGEON ROOST STATE HISTORIC SITE
(5 miles south of Scottsburg on US 31)
Scottsburg 47170

- ❑ Phone: (812) 265-3526, **Web: www.in.gov/ism/sites/pigeonroost/**
- ❑ Hours: Open dawn to dusk.
- ❑ Admission: FREE, donations accepted.

The site is a 44 foot limestone monument memorializing 24 settlers killed during an 1812 raid. The immediate result of the Pigeon Roost conflict was the effect it had on settlers. Fearing further attacks, communities surrounding Pigeon Roost moved into forts and blockhouses. Settlers planned more militia raids on Native American settlements across the Indiana Territory. Skirmishes between settlers and tribes continued until the Treaty of Ghent was signed in 1814 ending the War of 1812.

FOREST DISCOVERY CENTER

533 Louis Smith Road (I – 64 exit 119. Follow signs for Hubers)

Starlight 47106

- ❑ Phone: (812) 923-1590, **Web: www.forestcenter.com**
- ❑ Hours: Tuesday-Saturday 9:00am-5:00pm, Sunday 1:00-5:00pm. EST
- ❑ Admission: $5.50 adult, $4.50 senior (55+), $3.00 child (6 –12)
- ❑ Tours: Every ½ hour
- ❑ Miscellaneous: Gift shop with wood artwork, toys, souvenirs.

As you enter from the lobby you'll explore the unique indoor forest made from wood products, complete with forest sounds (birds, brush). It's hard to tell it isn't really indoor forest trees! Before heading upstairs, view the short orientation film narrated by Oakie Acorn. Once upstairs, you can walk through an enormous giant oak tree where you can view videos and sign the tree in support of re-forestation efforts. Next, gaze at the 1000 sq. ft. mural created from small wood inlays using age-old techniques called "marquetry". Artisans are usually available to show you how it was done. A glass enclosed skywalk brings you to a real, working company rough mill. Arrows and signs describe how logs become trimmed and molded. They don't waste anything...even the sawdust left over is burned as fuel for the electric generators. Defective wood chunks are made into mulch. The 13 step process begins with sawed logs, then dried in kilns to remove moisture, then planed, then electronically cut and finally jointed or sorted by size of "clear" (non-defective) board.

STARVE HOLLOW STATE FOREST

4345 South CR 275 West

Vallonia 47281

❑   Phone: (812) 358-3464
     Web: www.state.in.us/dnr/forestry/property/starvhlw.htm

Volleyball, Softball & Basketball, Fishing on the 145 acre lake, Swimming.

VERSAILLES STATE PARK

Box 205, US 50

Versailles 47042

❑   Phone: (812) 689-6424
     Web: www.in.gov/dnr/parklake/parks/versailles.html
❑   Admission: $3.00-$5.00 per vehicle.

Relax while fishing on the 230-acre lake where you can rent a paddleboat, rowboat or canoe. Bring your bicycle and pedal the nearby 27-mile Hoosier Hills Bicycle Route. Also Bridle Trails, Swimming / Pool and waterslide.

Chapter 8

South West Area

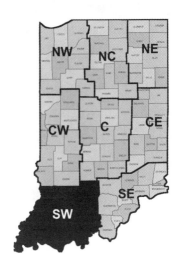

148

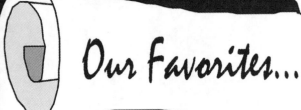

Our Favorites...

Grouseland

Evansville Museum of Arts,
History & Science

Angel Mounds Historic Site

Indiana Territory Capitol Village

Log Inn

Turner Doll Factory

Inside Prehistoric Indian Dwelling

ANTIQUE AUTO & RACE CAR MUSEUM

3348 16th Street (Stone City Mall)

Bedford 47421

- ❑   Phone: (812) 275-0556, **Web: www.autoracemuseum.com**
- ❑   Hours: Monday-Saturday Noon-6:00pm (April-December).
  Extended Summer Hours.
- ❑   Admission: $3.00 day pass, $5.00 yearly pass.

There are over 130 cars on display at the museum. Exhibits include Indy 500 Race Cars, Classics, Model A & T Fords, Sprint Cars, Midgets & ¼ Midget Race Cars, Nascar, and Special Interest Cars, including Plymouth Superbirds, Mustangs, Camaros, Chevelles, & Corvettes. Also, vintage and current racing videos.

BLUESPRING CAVERNS PARK

1459 Bluespring Caverns Rd (US 50 and SR 37 on CR 450 South)

Bedford 47421

- ❑   Phone: (812) 279-9471, **Web: www.bluespringscaverns.com**
- ❑   Hours: Daily 9:00am-5:00pm. (Memorial Day-Labor Day),
  Weekends only (April, May, September & October) EST.
- ❑   Admission: $10.00 adult, $5.00 child (3-15)
- ❑   Miscellaneous: Always a 52 degree constant temperature – a light
  jacket recommended. Myst'ry River Gemstone Mine – prospect
  for your own gemstones. "Overnight Adventures" for organized
  youth groups.

Years ago the White River cut into small cracks in limestone rock and dissolved it forming cave passages. As glaciers moved into the area they brought debris of soil and rock that were deposited. In the 1940's, a large pond on a farm disappeared overnight to reveal the entrance to the cave. The Myst'ry River tour boat glides along the quiet waters into the heart of a subterranean natural world. The guide will point out unusual formations and the interesting albino blind fish and crawfish that live in darkness.

HOOSIER STATE FOREST

811 Constitution Avenue (Brownstown Ranger District)

Bedford 47421

❑ Phone: (812) 275-5987 (Brownstown) and (812) 547-7051 (Tell City Ranger), **Web: www.fs.fed.us/r9/hoosier**

Situated in the rolling hills of south central Indiana, the Hoosier hides its geologic landscapes beneath a canopy of hickory and oak. A little exploration reveals a landscape of underground rivers, caves, sinkholes, box canyons, limestone bluffs, and narrow ridges. The most popular spots are:

❑ WATCHABLE WILDLIFE SITES - Buzzard Roost Overlook is located approximately two miles north of Magnet.

❑ CHARLES C. DEAM WILDERNESS - Indiana's only Congressionally designated wilderness area has 13,000 acres providing for solitude and a remote experience.

❑ HICKORY RIDGE LOOKOUT TOWER - Constructed by the CCC in 1939.

❑ PIONEER MOTHERS MEMORIAL FOREST - An 88 acre virgin old-growth forest and archaeological site. Explore virgin forest of ancient oaks and 130-foot walnut trees with 42-inch diameters.

❑ LICK CREEK SETTLEMENT - site of a 1815-1900 African American settlement.

❑ HEMLOCK CLIFFS - a box-shaped canyon with sandstone formations, seasonal water falls and rock shelters. And, of course, the canyon's cool climate is perfect for hemlock -- these tall evergreens with short needles and small cones simply thrive in this environment and so will you. Hemlock Cliffs is located west of Highway 37 about two miles north of Interstate 64.

❑ RICKENBAUGH HOUSE - A stone house built in 1874, used as a local post office and church meeting house.

❑ SUNDANCE LAKE - a 5 acre lake named for a Native American spiritual dance held annually near the site.

❑   <u>CLOVER LICK BARRENS</u> - Shallow soils and rock outcrops are found in these prairie-like, fire-dependant ecosystems which have many rare species.

❑   <u>WESLEY CHAPEL GULF</u> - This National Natural Landmark is an 8 acre collapsed sinkhole with a floor which provides a window to the underground river system.

❑   <u>BUFFALO TRACE</u> - an historic pathway used by migrating buffalo from the Falls of the Ohio River near Louisville to Vincennes where they crossed into the Illinois prairie.

❑   <u>TIPSHAW LAKE BEACH</u>

The Ohio River and the forest's four lakes offer a little something for everyone, including swimming, waterfowl viewing, canoeing, boating, and fishing for catfish and bass.

TURNER DOLL FACTORY

RR 1, Heltonville - Bartlettsville Road (Highway 50, best to call for directions or get off website)

Bedford (Heltonville) 47436

❑   Phone: (812) 834-6692; (800) 887-6372
Web: www.turnerdolls.com

❑   Hours: Monday-Friday 10:00am-5:00pm, Saturday 10:00am-4:00pm.

❑   Admission: FREE

❑   Tours: Monday-Friday 9:00am-3:00 pm.

❑   Miscellaneous: Gift Shop with over-run discounted dolls. Located on farm property so the non-doll lovers can wander outside to see the variety of animals. They will send you a map to the exact location of property.

How are dolls' eyes popped in? This, and many questions you wouldn't even think to ask are answered during this delightfully explained tour. The vinyl parts of a doll are made with liquid that looks like thick, light chocolate milk. Liquid vinyl is poured into the mold of a head, arm or leg and then put in a rotating oven. How do they get the vinyl to coat just the outside of the mold and not fill the inside? Artists hand-paint the faces and add accents of blush (with an airbrush) to certain parts of the arms and legs to make them look real. Next, the doll is assembled and stuffed with "fluff" and beads in just the right places so when you hold the baby doll, it feels real! Each doll has its own name and outfit (hand-sewn by locals). Our favorite is the "Kradle Kids" collection - they have such cute "pouty faces".

PATOKA LAKE STATE RESERVOIR

RR 1

Birdseye 47513

❑   Phone: (812) 685-2464 or (812) 547-7028
     Web: www.explore-si.com/PatokaLake.html

Archery range, Frisbee Golf Course, Solar Heated Visitors Center (illustrated displays on wildlife, history, birds of prey, solar energy and the viewing of a live bald eagle are all part of the Center's Raptor Education Program), house-boating, water-skiing, swimming, and fishing. Large campgrounds, launching ramps, marina, paved biking trails and a large supervised beach and swimming (Memorial to Labor Day). Lodging is available at cozy cabins and rustic chalets near or on the lake.

PERRY COUNTY MUSEUM

PO Box 36 (Seventh & Taylor Streets, old County Courthouse)

Cannelton 47520

❑   Phone: (812) 547-3190
     Web: www.perrycountyindiana.org/attract/pccourthouse.html
❑   Hours: Sunday 1:00-4:00pm and by appointment.

Early Perry County life is set in displays of the following: Coal-Clay - Cotton Textile Industries, Native American Artifacts, Civil War and Other War Memorabilia, Perry County Fossils and Minerals, Blacksmith Shop - Carpenter's Shop - Stone Mason's exhibit, "The Victorian Parlor" of 1870, and a media center on military, river history and steamboats.

DR. TED'S MUSICAL MARVELS
RR 2, Box 30A (I-64 exit 57 to US 231 North)
Dale 47523

- ❏ Phone: (812) 937-4250
- ❏ Hours: Monday-Saturday 10:00am-6:00pm, Sunday 1:00-6:00pm (Memorial Day-Labor Day). Weekends only in May & September.
- ❏ Admission: Adults $4.50, Children $2.00 (6-12)
- ❏ Tours:
- ❏ Miscellaneous: Gift shop

Take a guided tour of wonderful collection of restored mechanical musical instruments including music boxes, street organs, nickelodeons. Takes you back in time to the hey day of amusement parks and carousels. Actually, hear them played.   Bring the grandparents along, for sure, on this trip.

GRAHAM FARMS CHEESE
State Route 57 North
Elnora 47529

- ❏ Phone: (812) 692-5237 or (800) 472-9178
  Web: www.grahamcheese.com
- ❏ Hours: Monday-Saturday 8:00am-6:00pm, Sunday Noon-5:00pm.
- ❏ Admission: FREE
- ❏ Tours: Best times for a tour are Monday, Wednesday, and Friday before 11:00am. These are the days they are making cheese. They will do tours on Tuesday and Thursday, but will consist of seeing the machinery only. Tours last approximately 15 minutes. They do have a ten minute video playing in the store in case you miss the tour.

View cheesemaking (they've been making it since 1928). Cheese sampling. Ask how early Amish farmers brought their raw milk in the morning. Purdue and State of Indiana cheeses are a must souvenir.

WESSELMAN WOODS NATURE PRESERVE

551 North Boeke Road (I-164 to SR 66)

Evansville 47711

- ☐ Phone: (812) 479-0771
  Web: www.wesselman.evansville.net/index.htm
- ☐ Hours: Trails - 7:00am-7:00pm (April-September), 8:00am-4:00pm (October-March). Nature Center - 9:00am-5:00pm (April-September), 8:00am-4:00pm (October-March). Closed Mondays and Thanksgivingtime, Christmastime, New Years.
- ☐ Admission: FREE

An ancient forest with 200 acres of bottomland hardwood forest, fields and ponds. The Nature Center has trail maps, lists of wildflowers, birds and trees to look for and brochures covering maple sugaring, pioneer skills and forestry. The preserve - where you can also find a section of the historic Wabash & Erie Canal - is home to myriad wildflowers, deer, birds, and a host of other wildlife. Stop by the Nature Center and leaf through exhibits and a wildlife observation room.

EVANSVILLE MUSEUM OF ARTS, HISTORY AND SCIENCE

411 SE Riverside Drive (Downtown in Sunset Park)

Evansville 47713

- ☐ Phone: (812) 425-2406, **Web: www.emuseum.org**
- ☐ Hours: Tuesday-Saturday 10:00am-5:00pm. Sunday Noon-5:00pm. CDT. Closed on New Year's Day, Memorial Day, Easter Sunday, Independence Day, Labor Day, Thanksgiving, Christmas Eve and Christmas Day.
- ☐ Admission: $2.00 adult, $1.00 child. EMTRAC admission $2.00 adult. Children under 12 are free if accompanied by an adult. Admission to Koch Planetarium $2.50 adult, $1.50 child (3-12).

❏   Miscellaneous: Museum Shop. Collection of artwork from the
      16th century to the present and an Anthropology gallery on the
      two upper levels. Koch Planetarium has "themed" programs
      weekly.

Explore prehistoric, Native American and Main Street (late 1800's)
History. Old-style tools they used, types of buildings they lived in,
and what the kids played with back then. The Science Center for
school-aged and pre-school kids has hands-on exhibits dealing
with lasers, optical illusions, gravity and spatial relationships - all
very applicable to everyday situations. Many "theme" exhibits
focus on subjects like weather or the "art of science". The
Transportation Center (outside) – "EMTRAC" focuses on modes
of early transport - dugout canals, steam boats, autos, and steam
locomotives.

ANGEL MOUNDS STATE HISTORIC SITE

8215 Pollack Avenue (I -164 to Highway 662, Covert Avenue Exit)

Evansville 47715

❏   Phone: (812) 853-3956, **Web: www.angelmounds.org**
❏   Hours: Tuesday-Saturday 9:00am - 5:00pm, Sunday and
      Holidays, 1:00-5:00pm (mid-March to mid-December)
❏   Admission: Donations
❏   Miscellaneous: Interpretive Center. Nature preserve. Picnic Area.

Located on the banks of the Ohio River, this is a well-preserved
prehistoric Indian settlement of the Mississippians who planted
corn, hunted and fished for food in the area for over 250 years. The
Indians had 1000 - 3000 people populate the area. 11 earthen
mounds served as elevated buildings until mysteriously abandoned.
The site also includes reconstructed winter houses, a round house,
summer houses, a stockade and a temple that formed a village
within the mounds. Learn about home and fortress construction -
do you know what "waffle" and "daub" mean?-- (twigs woven
between logs, then plastered with clay). The Middle-Mississippi
tribe were known for their pottery and animal-shaped toys made
from clay with added crushed mussel shells (used as a tempering

agent). A popular kids game called "chunky" is played by throwing spears at small rolling stone discs. The closest spear wins. The earthen, thatched living huts had heating and air-conditioning - how?

HANDS ON DISCOVERY CHILDREN'S MUSEUM

Washington Square Mall, 1102 South Green River Rd (next to Sears)

Evansville 47715

- ❑   Phone: (812) 477-4929, **Web: www.handsondiscovery.org**
- ❑   Hours: Fridays & Saturdays 10:00am-5:00pm, Sundays Noon-5:00pm.
- ❑   Admission: $3.00 general (ages 2+)

A place for kids ages 2-12 and their adults where children "play to learn" and adults "learn to play". Learn about health and nutrition with Stuffee; pretend you're on a TV news set; see Seascape ocean creatures; pretend to have a meal at the International Diner; play music or perform; Touch the Future in the NASA galaxy; importance of thumbs and healthy teeth; computer and the arts; or finish in the Rain Forest or Fantasy Forest play areas (how about all that rice?).

MESKER PARK ZOO AND BOTANIC GARDEN

2421 Bement Avenue (off SR 66, Mesker Park)

Evansville 47720

- ❑   Phone: (812) 428-0715, **Web: www.meskerparkzoo.com**
- ❑   Hours: Daily 9:00am-4:00pm (Summer - Weekends and Holidays until 7:00 pm).
- ❑   Admission: $4.00-$5.00 (ages 3+)

The rolling hills of this 70 some acres are home to approximately 600 animals. Indiana's largest zoo includes a petting zoo, zoo train, Lake Victoria paddle boat rides, Discovery Center rain forest and

Jungle Cafe. Resident monkeys live in the center of a lake in a concrete replica of Christopher Columbus' Santa Maria. The zoo is divided into the African Panorama, Tropical Americas, Asian Valley, Lemur Forest, and North America forest - including lions and a tiger, birds of all feathers, monkeys and lemurs, gazelle and giraffe, kangaroos and kudus, leopards and a warthog, zebras & zebus.

PIKE STATE FOREST
6583 East SR 364
Ferdinand 47532

❏   Phone: (812) 367-1524
    Web: www.state.in.us/dnr/forestry/property/pike.htm

Topography at Pike State Forest varies from hilly uplands to the low bottomlands of the Patoka River. Because of the diversity of sites, a wide variety of plant and animal life make their homes at Pike. Several recreational opportunities are available at Pike State Forest, including hunting, horseback riding, picnicking, bird watching and hiking.

FRENCH LICK SPRINGS RESORT
8670 West State Road 56
French Lick 47432

❏   Phone: (800) 457-4042 reservations or (812) 936-9300
    Web: www.frenchlick.com

Reasonable resort accommodations with kid-friendly activities like: Archery, Badminton, Basketball, Bike Rental, Bingo, Board Games, Boating (Patoka Lake), Bowling, Croquet, Fishing (Patoka Lake), Golf, Horseback Riding, Miniature Golf, Playground, Kids Club with childcare and planned activities, Playground, Nature Hikes, Pony Rides, Rec Center (arcade), Skiing (Paoli Peaks), Surrey Rides, Swimming (indoor/outdoor), Tennis (indoor /outdoor), Train Rides (IN Railway Museum), Trolley Rides and

Volleyball. Some activities are available during season (May - October) only. Availability of some activities is subject to weather conditions. Many activities charge separate fees. Parents can play golf or go to the spa springs treatments while kids are at the Kids Club.

INDIANA RAILWAY MUSEUM AND TRAIN RIDES

SR 56, 1 Monon Street

French Lick 47432

- ❑ Phone: (812) 936-2405 or (800) 74-TRAIN
  Web: www.geocities.com/TheTropics/Beach/5285
- ❑ Hours: Weekends and Holidays 10:00am, 1:00pm & 4:00 pm. (April-October)
- ❑ Admission: $8.00 adult, $4.00 child (3-11)
- ❑ Tours: 2 hour, 20 mile train trip.
- ❑ Miscellaneous: Train Robbery Rides on Memorial Day, July 4th and Labor Day weekends. Gift Shop and snacks.

The museum displays diesel and steam locomotives, a rare railway Post Office car and a 1951 dining car. The Springs Valley Electric Trolley (shortest trolley line in the world) carries passengers for a little ride for a little fee ($1-2.00). Take the Train Ride through 20 miles of Hoosier National Forest and the 2200 ft. Burton Tunnel (one of the longest railroad tunnels in the state). The area's history is related by uniformed crew members - many who have personal stories to tell.

COLONEL WILLIAM JONES STATE HISTORIC SITE

Rte. 1, Box 600 (one mile west of US 231 on Boone Street)

Gentryville 47537

- ❑ Phone: (812) 937-2802, **Web: www.state.in.us/ism/sites/jones/**

- ❑ Hours: Wednesday-Saturday 9:00am-5:00pm, Sunday 1:00-5:00pm (mid-March to mid-December). Closed on Thanksgiving, Christmastime, New Year's and Easter.
- ❑ Admission: FREE. Donations accepted.
- ❑ Miscellaneous: Situated on 100 acres of forest, it also offers a self-guiding nature trail, picnic area and a restored log barn.

This carefully restored 1834 Federal-design home of the merchant employer of Abraham Lincoln offers a unique look at the early development of Indiana and the life of Colonel William Jones, who was also a politician, farmer and soldier. The home includes guided tours, themed talks, and exhibits.

LOG INN

Old State Rd (RR 2, I-64 to US 41 East)

Haubstadt 47639

- ❑ Phone: (812) 867-3216
- ❑ Hours: Tuesday-Thursday 4:00-9:00pm, Friday-Saturday 4:00-10:00pm.
- ❑ Admission: Around $10.00 adult, $5.00 child for Family Style Dinners.

Built in 1825 as a Noon Day Stage Coach Stop and Trading Post. Dine in the same original Log Room that Abraham Lincoln stopped at in November, 1844 enroute back from visiting his mother's grave. It was part of his campaign speaking tour. Officially recognized as the oldest restaurant in Indiana, authentic 1-foot thick logs surround you as you eat their wonderful fried chicken meals. Take time to read the articles on the walls while you wait for dinner. Dinners served by a la carte menu or family style.

DUBOIS COUNTY MUSEUM

1103 Main Street (Gramelspacher-Gutzweiler Bldg.)

Jasper 47546

❑   Phone: (812) 634-7733 or (800) 968-4578
     Web: www.duboiscounty.org
❑   Hours: Friday and Saturday 10:00am-2:00pm, Sunday 1:00-
     4:00pm. EST
❑   Admission: FREE. Donations accepted.

The Museum traces the region's dynamic history from the Ice Age
to the present. Archaic Indians roamed the forests and glens that
once blanketed this land. They were followed by the Piankshaw
Indians, who preceded the Scots-Irish settlers. An overwhelming
migration of Germans arrived in the Mid-Nineteenth Century. Visit
a log cabin home of early settlers, stop by the Mercantile for some
fashion tips, and also discover the death rituals of the early people.

INDIANA BASEBALL HALL OF FAME

1436 Leopold Street, Hwy. 162 & College Avenue (Campus of
Vincennes Univ. - Jasper, Ruxer Student Center)

Jasper 47546

❑   Phone: (812) 482-2262, **Web: www.indbaseballhalloffame.org**
❑   Hours: Monday-Friday 9:00am-5:00pm, Saturday-Sunday
     11:00am-3:00pm (August-June). Daily 11:00am-3:00pm
     (Summers). Closed legal holidays.

The sponsoring body of the hall of fame is the Indiana High School
Baseball Coaches Association, IHSBCA, which has served the
baseball coaches of Indiana since 1971. The first inductions were
in July 1979 and there are currently 91 inductees in the hall of
fame in four categories: pro-player, coach-manager (high school,
college, pro), contributor and veteran.

WYANDOTTE CAVES

7315 S. Wyandotte Cave Rd. (I-64 to SR 66 South to SR 62 East)

Leavenworth 47137

❑   Phone: (812) 738-2782, **Web: www.cccn.net**
❑   Hours: Daily 9:00am-5:00pm. EDST. Closed Mondays in
       winter (mid-September to mid-May)
❑   Admission:$5.00-7.00 adult, $3.00-4.00 child
❑   Tours: 30 minute to 2 hour trips
❑   Miscellaneous: Children 12 and under must be with an adult.
       Caves are a constant 52 degrees.

Reservations must be made for a guided 3, 5 or 7 hour tour. These
tours offer serious spelunkers a real challenge with several long
crawls and some climbing. Lights and helmets are provided, as are
lockers and shower facilities.

  • <u>LITTLE WYANDOTTE TOUR</u> – short and easy with
     flowstone and dripstone formations. Indirect electrical
     lighting. 1/2 mile, 30-45 minute tour.
  • <u>BIG WYANDOTTE HISTORICAL TOURS</u> – Rugged
     Mountain, geologic historical formations. Summer only.
     Prehistoric Indian "rooms" and "hallways".
  • <u>MONUMENT MOUNTAIN TOUR</u> – deep cave with
     formations like helictites, gypsum/flint quarries. 1 1/2
     miles of steep terrain and stairs in lighted passageways.

BUFFALO RUN GRILL & GIFTS

Highway 162

Lincoln City 47552

❑   Phone: (812) 937-2799
❑   Hours: Daily, except Tuesday 11:00am-7:00pm CDT (Memorial
       Day-Labor Day). Saturday/Sunday 10:00am-7:00pm CST (Labor
       Day to mid-December).

Buffalo Run Grill & Gifts offers buffalo and ostrich burgers which are lower in fat than turkey. Live buffalo and ostrich can be seen grazing behind the business. Experience the sights of true pioneer living with buffalo roaming behind a frontier encampment (during special seasonal events). Frontier crafts, demonstrations and trading goods are available along with bison products in the gift shop. Farm tours are also available with pre-tour reservation or during special events.

LINCOLN BOYHOOD NATIONAL MEMORIAL

SR 162 (2 miles East of Gentryville off I-64)

Lincoln City 47552

- ❑   Phone: (812) 937-4541, **Web: www.nps.gov/libo/**
- ❑   Hours: Daily 8:00am-5:00pm. The farm is staffed from mid-April through September full time, and intermittently in October.
- ❑   Admission: $2.00 general, $4.00 family.
- ❑   Miscellaneous: Picnic Shelter.

The Visitor Center is a museum with film "Here I Grew Up" (from age 7-21 years) - young Abe Lincoln. The Cabin site is a working pioneer farmstead with animals and crops where Abraham used to split rails, plant and plow or milk cows. See his mother's grave (she died of "milksick" when he was 9 years old). We learned that "milksick" is a disease caused by poisonous milk produced by cows that eat snakeroot (if pastures are dry, cows migrate to forest areas where poisonous plants grow). Walk on the Boyhood Nature Trails - the same trails that a young Abraham would have walked alone in thought years ago.

YOUNG ABE LINCOLN MUSICAL DRAMA/ LINCOLN STATE PARK

Lincoln State Park Amphitheatre (I-64, Exit 57 to US 231 South)

Lincoln City 47552

❑ Phone: (812) 937-4710 (park) or (800) 264-4223
Web: www.lincoln-amphitheatre.com
❑ Hours: Wednesday-Sunday 1:30 pm and 7:30 pm CDT .
Reservations best. (mid-June to mid-August). See website for
schedule of which play is showing each night. They show one
other drama each summer on alternate days.
❑ Admission: $15.00 adults, $13.00 senior (60+), $8.00 child
(under 18).
❑ Tours: Backstage $2.00/person before shows.
❑ Miscellaneous: Sunday Family Night is $8.00/person. Kid's Day
Special Price $6.00/person. Completely covered amphitheatre.
No rainchecks.

See the Story of Lincoln's Youth in Southern Indiana. Relive the
early 1800's on the Indiana frontier as over 40 actors become (very
believable) Lincoln family and friends. See him deal with the death
of his mother and sister and his first brush with slavery. Experience
the touching, funny and serious sides of youth that developed him
into a well respected man. Lincoln State Park is a scenic 1,747-
acre park established in 1932 as a memorial to Nancy Hanks
Lincoln. Recreational facilities include Lake Lincoln, lakeside
shelter house, boat rental building, nature center, cabins, picnic
areas, shelters and trails, plus Class A and primitive camp sites.

CAVE COUNTRY CANOES - BLUE RIVER

PO Box 217, 112 Main Street

Marengo 47140

❑ Phone: (812) 365-2705, **Web: www.cavecountrycanoes.com**
❑ Season: (April-October)
❑ Admission: $16.00-$19.00 per person.

Cave Country Canoes (cont.)

❑   Tours: Half day (2-4 hours) and Full day (4-7 hours) trips,
      guided. All rates include paddle, lifejacket, map and
      transportation.

Two bases to serve you... Milltown & Leavenworth. Enjoy canoes,
kayaks & shuttle service on the Blue River ... the most spring fed
of all Indiana's streams. The many springs account for the aqua-
blue color of the river, leading to the name "The Blue". In many
areas limestone bluffs, dotted with cave entrances, tower above the
river attesting to the fact that "The Blue" flows through the heart of
Indiana's Cave Country. The river valley is noted for its abundant
wildlife, natural beauty, and excellent fishing.

MARENGO CAVE

PO Box 217 (I – 64 to SR 66 and SR 64)

Marengo 47140

❑   Phone: (812) 365-2705, **Web: www.marengocave.com**
❑   Hours: Daily 9:00 am-6:00 pm. (Summer). 9:30am-5:30pm
      (Spring and Fall). 9:00am-5:00 pm (Winter). Closed Christmas
      and Thanksgiving Day. EST
❑   Admission: $11.00-$12.00 adult, Half-price fee child (4–12).
      Combine tours and save $3-$6.00 per person.
❑   Tours: Leave every 30 minutes
❑   Miscellaneous: Hungry Grotto Snack Shop. Cave Springs
      Mining Company – gemstone mining – Daily (April-October).
      Climbing Tower. Canoe trips, trail rides. Camping.

Tours include:

❑   CRYSTAL PALACE TOUR – 40 minutes, world famous
      "Crystal Palace" cave room with dramatic lighting presentation.
      Mountain rooms and massive deposits.
❑   DRIPSTONE TRAIL TOUR – One hour and 10 minutes.
      Known for soda straw formations, slender and intricate
      "dripping" deposits. Includes "Pulpit Rock", "Music Hall" and
      "Penny Ceiling".

❑   THE CRAWL – challenging, simulated cave maze crawl. Do
    you have what it takes to be a cave explorer? Physically fit ages
    8 – 30 only. Claustrophobia City! Best to try before the Cave
    Exploring trip is purchased.
❑   CAVE EXPLORING TRIPS – age 10 and up. Don a lighted
    helmet and old clothes and crawl through undeveloped new cave
    passages. Be sure to get a picture of yourself on this excursion.
    Friends won't believe it!

SPRING MILL STATE PARK

PO Box 376 (SR 37 to SR 60 East)

Mitchell 47446

❑   Phone: (812) 849-4129
    Web: www.in.gov/dnr/parklake/parks/springmill.html
❑   Admission: $3.00-$5.00 per vehicle.

Lots to do and see here...Beginning with the Spring Mill Inn (812)
849-4081 - Accommodations and Restaurant. Tour the restored
Pioneer Village including a gristmill, lime kiln, sawmill, hat shop,
post office, apothecary and boot shop. Plan to take a boat ride into
Twin Caves (tour times are assigned daily, they are seasonal) or
walk into Donaldson cave. Grissom Memorial honors Hoosier
astronaut "Gus" Grissom, one of seven Mercury astronauts and
America's second man in space (space capsule and video of space
exploration). Other facilities include: Indoor Swimming/Pool,
Tennis & other games, Camping, Cultural Arts Programs, Fishing /
Ice Fishing, Hiking Trails, Nature Center / Interpretive Services,
and a Saddle Barn.

GASTOF AMISH VILLAGE RESTAURANT

City Road 650 East (off US 150)

Montgomery 47558

- ❑ Phone: (812) 486-3977 or (812) 486-2600
- ❑ Hours: Monday-Saturday. Lunch/Dinner. Breakfast Tuesday, Wednesday, & Saturday only.
- ❑ Tours: By buggy past a harness shop, quilt and craft shop, general store and candy factory.
- ❑ Miscellaneous: Many "Amish" or "Harvest" Festivals held at site year-round.

The restaurant, built of Indiana oak and poplar, was framed by Amish carpenters with simple joints and pegs. Amish cooking.

HARMONIE STATE PARK

3451 Harmonie State Park Road (Off CR 69 - on the banks of the Wabash)

New Harmony 47631

- ❑ Phone: (812) 682-4821
  Web: www.in.gov/dnr/parklake/parks/harmonie.html
- ❑ Admission: $3.00-$5.00 per vehicle.

Located "on the banks of the Wabash," 25 miles northwest of Evansville, this park has a beautiful swimming pool, shady picnic areas, and ravines. Trails for walking, biking and nature hikes will lure you for a visit. They also have cabins and a Nature Center.

PAOLI PEAKS SKI & SNOWBOARD RESORT

2798 W. CR 25 S

Paoli 47454

- ❑ Phone: (812) 723-4696, **Web: www.skipeaks.com/home.html**

❑   Hours: Monday-Thursday 10:00am-9:30pm, Friday 10:00am-
      10:00pm and Friday & Saturday Midnight-6:00am, Saturday
      9:00am-10:00pm, Sunday 9:00am-9:30pm. See website for
      special holiday hours.

On the Slopes there is a natural hill with 300 ft. vertical drop.
Average grade: 10%-15%. Terrain: 25% beginner, 55%
intermediate, 10% advanced, 10% expert park. 1 quad chair, 3
triple chairs, 1 beginner double chair, 3 surface tows.

- **SKI LODGE** - 45,000 square ft. day lodge with self
  service restaurant & pizzeria, rentals and shops and ticket
  sales.
- **LODGING & ACCOMMODATIONS** - Condominiums
  next to the slopes, B&B's, cabins, motels, resort hotels.
- **KID'S SNOW CAMP** - All day supervision includes four
  hours of instruction and lunch. ages 4-12.

LINCOLN PIONEER VILLAGE & MUSEUM
416 Main Street (Rockport City Park, at west end of Main)
Rockport 47635

❑   Phone: (812) 649-4215, **Web:**
      www.spencerco.org/village/village.cfm
❑   Hours: Wednesday-Saturday 10:00am-5:00pm, Sunday 1:00-
      5:00pm (June-September) and by appointment.
❑   Admission: $2.00 suggested donation.

The Lincoln Pioneer Village Museum houses hundreds of
fascinating artifacts from the area's historic past including a hutch
made by Abraham Lincoln's father, Thomas. Located next to the
museum is the historic Lincoln Pioneer Village, consisting of
cabins that are replicas from the Lincoln era in Spencer County
(cabins may be seen by appointment- including the law office,
schoolhouse, church, store and typical cabin homes).

HOLIDAY WORLD THEME PARK AND SPLASHIN' SAFARI

452 E. Christmas Blvd (7 miles South of I-64, exit 63, Highway 162)

Santa Claus 47579

- ❑ Phone: (877) GO-FAMILY, **Web: www.holidayworld.com**
- ❑ Hours: Holiday World opens 10:00 am. Splashin' Safari 11:00 am. Closing varies by season. (May to mid-October)
- ❑ Admission: General range $22.00-28.00.
- ❑ Miscellaneous: Season passes and 2-day passes save money. Charge cards taken.

HOLIDAY WORLD is consistently rated as one of the cleanest amusement parks in the mid-West. Included in admission are Live shows (country, pop, high dive), Raging Rapids whitewater rafting ride, The Raven, The Legend or the Howlert coasters; Frightful Falls log flume ride; Costumed characters roam about in Holidog's Funtown; and Banshee six story weightlessness ride. Santa appears daily-look for him mostly in Rudolph's Ranch Kiddie Park.

SPLASHIN' SAFARI is where Certified lifeguards oversee fun areas like: Monsoon Lagoon-a 12 level interactive area with water effects, body slides and the GIANT bucket. WATCH OUT!; Congo River tube float; Zoombabwe - the largest waterslide in the world; Watubee whitewater ride; Speed slide, wave pool, covered slide; and Crocodile Isle - scaled-down pool and slides for the younger set.

MARTIN STATE FOREST

PO Box 599

Shoals 47581

- ❑ Phone: (812) 247-3491

  Web: www.state.in.us/dnr/forestry/property/martin.htm

Martin State Forest offers a variety of educational opportunities through its woodland management trail and arboretum. The forest features rugged hills, deep woods and long hiking trails.

FLOOD WALL MURAL AT SUNSET PARK

Sunset Park, Ohio River (Washington & 7th Street)

Tell City 47586

❑   Phone: (812) 547-7933

      Web: www.perrycountyindiana.org/attract/floodwall.html

Sunset park contains a painted mural on the flood wall. It was done in sections and took 3 years to paint, 1992 - 1994. It is a rendition of early days of Perry County. Each building, boat and person has historical significance. Each of ten panels has a theme such as manufacturing, lifestyle (residences), mills, banks, merchants and steamboats.

GEORGE ROGERS CLARK NATIONAL HISTORIC PARK

401 South 2nd Street

Vincennes 47591

❑   Phone: (812) 882-1776, **Web: www.nps.gov/gero**
❑   Hours: Daily 9:00am-5:00pm. Closed Thanksgiving, Christmas, New Years.
❑   Admission: $2.00 adult (age 17+).

The site of a little-known, but extremely important, battle that occurred during the Revolutionary War. On February 25, 1779 Virginian George Rogers Clark, with his small army of American frontiersmen and French inhabitants, captured Fort Sackville from the British. Clark's victory aided the United States in laying claim to the vast region that later became the Old Northwest Territory. Today a massive granite-and-marble memorial, more than 80 feet high, stands on the location of Fort Sackville and pays tribute to Clark and his men. Inside are Clark's words carved into Indiana limestone "Great things have been effected by a few men well conducted."

GROUSELAND

3 West Scott Street (Downtown at Park and Scott Streets)

Streets. Follow signs)

Vincennes 47591

- ❑ Phone: (812) 882-2096
  Web: http://users.bestonline.net/pwilk/grouseland.htm
- ❑ Hours: Daily 9:00am-5:00pm (except January, February 11:00am-4:00pm)
- ❑ Admission: $3.00 adult, $1-$2.00 child (under age 5 years)
- ❑ Tours: Ring the doorbell and a guide will escort you in.

The Home of William Henry Harrison, the first Governor of the Indiana Territory and later the 9th President of the United States. He died in office 31 days after his inauguration - some say unnecessarily due to blood letting. The dining room has a bullet hole in the window shutter where someone tried to shoot Harrison (they missed!). As you walk from upstairs down to the warming kitchen (do you know what a buttery is?), you'll see a cutaway of original flooring used in the home. The layers of clay and straw underneath wood provided insulation and noise protection (Harrison didn't want servants to eavesdrop). Stories for the kids include the "giant travel chest" and a Mother's apron needle used for more than sewing. Mr. Harrison is best known for his campaign against Tecumseh - The Treaty of Grouseland was signed at his home.

INDIANA MILITARY MUSEUM

4305 Old Bruceville Road

Vincennes 47591

- ❑ Phone: (812) 882-8668 or (800) 886-6443
  Web: www.nps.gov/gero
- ❑ Hours: Daily Noon-4:00pm. Winter hours vary.
- ❑ Admission: $2.00 adult, $1.00 student.

❑   Tours: Guided tours only by arrangement.

Military history from the Civil War to Desert Storm. Outdoors - tanks, artillery, helicopters. Indoors - uniforms, flags, relics from battlefields, captured enemy souvenirs, World War II toys and homefront items.

INDIANA TERRITORY CAPITOL VILLAGE

1 West Harrison Street (Downtown)

Vincennes 47591

❑   Phone: (812) 882-7472, **Web: www.in.gov/ism/sites/vincennes/**
❑   Hours: Wednesday-Saturday 9:00am-5:00pm, Sunday 1:00-
5:00pm (mid-March to mid-December)
❑   Admission: Donations $2.00 adult, $1.00 child
❑   Tours: Begin at Log Cabin Visitor's Center
❑   Miscellaneous: Videotape of Vincennes' history in the Visitor's
Center. OLD FRENCH HOUSE AND INDIAN MUSEUM is
nearby and exhibits pioneer life including influences of early
inhabitants, American Indian tribes.

Start at the oldest major government building in the Midwest - the Indiana Territory Capitol Building. Then, stop in for a demonstration of old-fashioned printing presses at the Elias Stout Print Shop...a replica print shop where they first printed the Law of the Territory and the first Territory newspaper, "The Indiana Gazette". Learn where we got the phrase, "UPPER CASE or capital letters" and "mind your P's and Q's". Lastly, step inside Maurice Thompson's birthplace where the author of "Alice of Old Vincennes" (a best-selling romance novel) was born. It features frame construction instead of logs and a cast iron stove in place of a drafty fireplace - both modern for the time.

DAVIESS COUNTY MUSEUM
Old Jefferson School (CR 150 South. Off SR 57)
Washington 47501

- ❑ Phone: (812) 254-5122
- ❑ Hours: Tuesday-Saturday 11:00am-3:00pm (October-April).
  Tuesday-Saturday 11:00am-4:00pm (May-September).
- ❑ Admission: Small (ages 12 +)
- ❑ Miscellaneous: Schools in area. Victorian furnishings and dolls,
  old license plates, church room, railroad room, medical room
  (early x-ray machine), military room, beauty/barber chair.

Seasonal &
Special Events

Chapter 9

*Note: **Pioneer Encampments** are listed in the back of this section.*

JANUARY

KIL-SO-QUEST SLED DOG RACE

NE – Huntington. Reservoir & Kilso-Quah Campground. (800) 848-4282. Indiana's only sled dog race! 2,3,4 and 6 dog races. No admission. (January, third weekend)

FEBRUARY / MARCH

MAPLE SYRUP FESTIVALS

Learn how maple syrup is made from tree tapping to evaporator demonstrations. Taste sampling of food with syrup like pancakes and kettle popcorn. Pioneer music and games.

- ❏ **CE – New Castle**. 6025 North CR 100 East. (765) 836-4432. (February, beginning around Valentines Day).
- ❏ **CW – Rockville**. Parke County Fairgrounds and Billie Creek Village. (765) 569-5226 or **www.billiecreek.org**. Admission. (End of February/beginning of March)
- ❏ **CW – Terre Haute**. Prairie Creek Park. (812) 462-3391 or **www.terrehaute.com**. FREE (Month-long February)
- ❏ **NC – Wakarusa**. Downtown. (574) 862-4344. FREE (Last Friday / Saturday of March)
- ❏ **NE – LaGrange**. Maplewood Nature Center. (260) 463-4022. Admission. (3rd weekend in March)
- ❏ **SE – Salem**. Sugarbush Farm. (812) 967-4491. FREE
- ❏ **SW - Evansville**. Wesselman Woods Nature Preserve. (812) 479-0771. Admission. (Early March weekend)

ST. PATRICK'S DAY CELEBRATIONS

On or the week before St. Patrick's Day see a downtown lunchtime parade. "Wearin of the green" celebrations include Irish Dancing, food and music. No Admission.

❏   Participating towns: **Ireland, Rising Sun, South Bend.**

APRIL

EASTER EGG HUNTS

Egg hunts, party with Easter Bunny, egg decorating contests, Easter Bonnet contests. No Admission.

❏   Participating towns: **C – Indianapolis** Parks & Rec. (317) 327-0000; **CW – Cloverdale**, Cagles Mill Lake (765) 795-4576; **SE – Vevay** (800) HELLO-VV; **SW – Washington**, Gasthof Amish Village, CR 650E. (812) 486-2600.

MAY

THE 500 FESTIVALS

(Activities to celebrate the Indy 500 Race), **www.500festival.com**.

ANDERSON LITTLE 500 FESTIVAL & RACE

❏   **C – Anderson**. Various locations. (765) 640-2437. Big wheel race, concert, fireworks, sprint car race. Admission. (May, week before Memorial Day)

BANK ONE FESTIVAL & KIDS DAY

❏   **C – Indianapolis**. Monument Circle. (800) 638-4296. The city's largest outdoor festival for children with Big Wheel races (ages 2-5), carnival, arts and crafts, prizes. No Admission. except for race registrants. (Saturday before Memorial Day weekend.)

The 500 Festivals (cont.)

500 FESTIVAL COMMUNITY DAY

❑ **C – Indianapolis**. Motor Speedway. (800) 638-4296. Lap the track in your own vehicle. See Pit Row, Gasoline Alley, and the Tower Terrace. Driver's and mechanic's autographs. Admission. (Thursday before race)

500 FESTIVAL PARADE

❑ **C – Indianapolis**. Downtown. (800) 638-4296. Drivers, floats, marching bands, celebrities. Admission for reserved seating. (Noon the day before race)

INDIANAPOLIS 500 MILE RACE

❑ **C – Indianapolis**. Motor Speedway. (800) 638-4296. The world's largest one-day sporting event. Admission. (Memorial Day)

ETHNIC FESTIVAL

NC – Goshen. Goshen College. **www.goshen.edu/events/ethnicfair**. (574) 535-7566. International Café, Markets of the World, entertainment, ethnic food. (May, first weekend)

FAMILY FUN FESTIVAL

NW – Cutler. Adams Mill. (765) 463-7893. Mill tours, old-fashioned games, hayrides, pony rides. FREE. (May, mid-month Sunday)

WHISTLE STOP DAYS

NW – Hesston. Hesston Steam Museum. (219) 872-5055. Ride three steam railroads, visit operating steam sawmill, steam crane, steam power plant and more. FREE. (May, last long weekend)

HARRISON COUNTY POPCORN FESTIVAL

SE – Corydon. Courthouse Square. (888) 738-2137. Celebrate the county's popcorn industry. Parade, popcorn demos and contests, popcorn-related foods. FREE. (May, mid-month weekend)

WINGS OVER MUSCATATUCK

SE – Seymour. Muscatatuck Nat'l Wildlife Refuge, US 50. (888) 524-1914. Indiana's only International Migratory Bird Festival – celebrating birds and the natural environment. Field trips, guided bird walks, bird crafts, bird photography, bird calling, tracking, puppet shows. Admission for field trips. (May, second long weekend)

KITE DAY

SW – Evansville. (812) 853-3956. A day of family fun with food, games and kites, kites, kites. (May, last Sunday)

JUNE

STRAWBERRY FESTIVALS

Sample strawberry treats like fresh strawberry shortcakes and strawberry ice cream or sundaes. Entertainment. Kids activities.

- ❑ **CE – Metamora**. Along the canal. (765) 647-2109. **www.metamora.com**. FREE. (June, first weekend)
- ❑ **CW – Crawfordsville**. Historic Lane Place. (800) 866-3973. **www.crawfordsville.org**. FREE. (June, second weekend)
- ❑ **CW– Lafayette**. YWCA, 6th & Cincinnati Streets. (765) 742-0075. Admission. (June, first Saturday)
- ❑ **CW – Terre Haute**. Downtown. (812) 533-1596. Admission. (June, third Saturday)
- ❑ **NC – Wabash**. Historic Downtown. Very Berry Strawberry Fest. (260) 563-1168. FREE. (June, second Saturday)
- ❑ **SE – Starlight**. St. John's Church. (812) 923-5785. FREE. (May, Last Saturday)

JUNE (cont.)

BILL MONROE MEMORIAL BEAN BLOSSOM BLUEGRASS FESTIVAL

C – Bean Blossom. Bluegrass Hall or Fame Museum. (800) 414-4677. **www.beanblossom.com**. The longest continuously running bluegrass festival in the world, held outdoors with six days of the best in bluegrass, featuring 25 bands, band contest, artist workshops, crafts, children's workshops, pickin' and jammin', food. Camping, cabin rentals, fishing and hiking trails available. Admission. (June, third week)

ITALIAN STREET FESTIVAL

C – Indianapolis. Holy Rosary Church. (317) 636-4778. More than 25 Italian meats, pastas, salads, desserts. Church tours, entertainment. Admission. (June, first full weekend)

MIDDLE EASTERN FESTIVAL

C– Indianapolis. St. George Orthodox Church. (317) 547-9356. Authentic food, dancing, music, cultural displays, cooking demos, tours. Admission. (June, second weekend)

WILBUR WRIGHT FESTIVAL

CE – Millville. Wilbur Wright Birthplace & Museum, CR 750 East. (765) 332-2495. Home tours, outdoor life-size replica of the 1903 Wright Flyer, live entertainment, flea market, car show, sky divers, kite flying, remote-controlled planes, tours, beans and cornbread. Pork chop dinner Saturday. FREE. (June, third weekend)

TASTE OF TIPPECANOE

CW – Lafayette. Downtown, Riehle Plaza. (765) 423-2787. **www.lafayette-in.com**. Outdoor festival featuring six stages with live entertainment, 30 local restaurant vendors, Kid's Taste area, fireworks. Admission. (June, third Saturday)

GLASS FESTIVAL

NC – Greentown. Downtown. (765) 628-6206. This town's birthday features tours of the glass factory (see chocolate glass), re-enactors, historical displays, children's activities, food, music, historical play. FREE. (June, second weekend)

EGG FESTIVAL

NC– Mentone. Menser Park. (574) 353-7417. The egg basket of the Midwest features the incredible edible egg in a parade, tractor pull, crafts, variety show. FREE. (June, first weekend)

COLE PORTER FESTIVAL

NC – Peru. Miami County Museum. (765) 473-9183. Cole Porter is celebrated as a native of this town with musical entertainment, memorabilia display, birthday cake and van tours. FREE. (June, second Saturday)

ROUND BARN FESTIVAL

NC – Rochester. Downtown, Main Street. (574) 224-2666. Bus tour of round barns and one-room school, bed races, rodeo, parade, kiddy races, wall rock climbing, food, entertainment, games. FREE. (June, second weekend).

ETHNIC FESTIVAL

NC – South Bend. Howard Park & East Race Waterway. (574) 299-4768. Variety of ethnic foods and entertainment. Children's activities and rides. FREE. (June, third weekend)

CITY OF LAKES BALLOONFEST

NC – Warsaw. Central Park, Winona Lake, and other locations. (800) 800-6090. Hot air balloons, evening balloon glow, sailboat regatta, concerts, fireworks, food. FREE. (June, last weekend)

GERMANFEST

NE – Fort Wayne. Headwaters Park Festival Center. (800) 767-7752 or **www.wunderbar.org**. German heritage celebrated with folk music, dancing, food, kindertag, sports, exhibitions. Admission. (June, third week)

JUNE (cont.)

GREEK FESTIVAL

NE – Fort Wayne. Headwaters Park. (260) 489-0774. Greek food, music, dancing and art. Admission. (June, last weekend)

RED, WHITE, & BLUE FESTIVAL

SE – Crothersville. Community School Grounds. (812) 793-3378. A patriotic salute to Flag Day includes a parade, hot air balloon race, carnival, entertainment. FREE. (June, second weekend)

DAVIESS COUNTY FAIR

SW – Elnora. Fairgrounds off SR57. (812) 692-5831. Family fun including demolition derbies, motorcycle thrill show, western horse show, rides, food, and nightly entertainment. (June, last week of month)

OFFICIAL INDIANA PICKIN' & FIDDLIN' CONTEST

SW – Petersburg. Prides Creek Park. **www.pikecountyin.org**. (812) 354-8155. State championships in fiddle, guitar, banjo, mandolin and harmonica. Old-time singing and bluegrass bands. Admission. (June, third weekend)

JULY

JULY 4TH CELEBRATIONS

Live entertainment, parade, carnival, food, fireworks.

- ❏ **C – Fishers**. A Glorious Fourth. Conner Prairie. (317) 776-6000 or **www.connerprairie.org**. Reading of the Declaration of Independence. Admission.
- ❏ **C – Indianapolis**. Fourth Fest. Downtown (317) 633-6363. FREE
- ❏ **C – Indianapolis**. Ice Cream Social. President Benjamin Harrison's Home. (317) 631-1898. Period costumed characters roam the grounds and talk to you. Admission.

- ❑ **CE – Metamora**. Old Fashioned 4th of July. Main Street. (765) 642-2194. FREE.
- ❑ **CW – Rockville**. July 4th Ice Cream Social. Billie Creek Village. (765) 569-3430. Grand cake walk. Admission.
- ❑ **NC – Elkhart**. Sky Concert. (800) 377-3579.
- ❑ **NE – Garrett**. Heritage Days. (260) 357-3133. Railroad Museum. (July 3rd & 4th)
- ❑ **NE – Geneva**, Amishville USA. (260) 589-3536.
- ❑ **NE – Huntington**. Forks of Wabash. (260) 356-1903.
- ❑ **NW – Crown Point. www.cpjuly4.com.** (July 4th)
- ❑ **NW – LaPorte**. Jaycees' 4th of July Celebration. (219) 324-5392. Over 50 years with fly over of military jets. Admission. Weeklong.
- ❑ **NW – Wolcott**. Wolcott House Grounds. (219) 279-2123. FREE. (July 3rd & 4th)
- ❑ **SE – Aurora**. Firecracker Festival. Lesko Park & Water Street. (812) 926-2625. FREE. (July, long weekend before July 4th)
- ❑ **SE – Corydon**. Old Settlers Day. Old Capitol Square. (812) 738-4890. Pioneer demonstrations. No Admission.
- ❑ **SW – Evansville**. Freedom Festival. Downtown riverfront. (812) 434-4848. Admission.

SCOTTISH FESTIVAL

C – Columbus. Mill Race Park. **www.scottishfestival.org**. (800) 468-6564 or Bagpipe bands, sheepdog trials, Highland dancing, athletic competitions and traditional foods. Admission. (July, third weekend)

HOT DOG FESTIVAL

C – Frankfort. Courthouse Square. (765) 654-4081. Hot dogs with every topping imaginable! Puppy Park with children's activities and other "dog" related events. FREE. (July, last weekend)

JULY (cont.)

ALOHA INTERNATIONAL

CE – Winchester. Willard Elementary School. (765) 584-6845. Hawaiian steel guitar artists from 26 states and several foreign countries perform. Grand Luau feast. Admission. (July, second weekend)

STEAM & GAS POWER FESTIVAL

CW – Battle Ground. Tippecanoe Battlefield. (765) 463-2828. **www.lafayette-in.com**. Antique tractor, steam and gas engines, threshing. Flea market, sawmill, spinning, quilting, wood carving, kiddie tractor pull. Tractor skill contest for all ages. Cross-cut saw contest, entertainment, food. Admission. (July, last long weekend)

WAAHPAAHSHIKI PEOPLES POW WOW

CW – Battle Ground. Tippecanoe Amphitheater Park. (765) 567-4000. **www.lafayette-in.com**. Intertribal pow wow, arts, food. Features Great Lakes Drums with hundreds of dancers. Admission. (July, second weekend)

ELKHART COUNTY 4-H FAIR

NC – Goshen, County Fairgrounds. (574) 533-3247 or **www.4hfair.org**. One of the largest county fairs in the nation with 4-H exhibits, demos, food, carnival and free top-name entertainment. Admission. (July)

HAYNES-APPERSON FESTIVAL

NC – Kokomo. Downtown. (800) 456-1106. The town celebrates its automotive history with Haynes Museum tours, car shows, a parade, carnival, food, and talent contest. FREE. (July, first weekend)

IRON HORSE FESTIVAL

NC – Logansport. Downtown. (574) 753-6388. Tour a railroad museum, train excursions, open cockpit plane rides. International food festival, parade. FREE. (July, mid-month weekend)

RIVERFEST CRUISE-IN

NC – Marion. Matter Park Shelter. (765) 668-4453. Family activities and entertainment surround a cruise-in with fireworks in the evening. (July 4th)

CIRCUS CITY FESTIVAL

NC – Peru. Circus City Festival Arena. (765) 472-3918 or **www.perucircus.com**. Best amateur youth performances include flying trapeze, high wire, bareback riding. Carnival downtown. Tour Hall of Fame, rides, food. Admission. (July, mid-month, weeklong)

SWISS DAYS

NE – Berne. Downtown. (260) 589-8080. Yodeling, folk dancing, concerts, cheese making factory tours, Swiss food and famous apple dumplings. FREE. (July, last weekend)

INDIANA HIGHLAND GAMES

NE – Fort Wayne. Zollner Stadium. (800) 767-7752. Sheep herding, bagpipes, Scottish dancing and food, competitions. Admission. (July, last Saturday)

THREE RIVERS FESTIVAL

NE – Fort Wayne. Headwaters Park. (260) 426-5556. Children's Fest, McDonald's Parade, music, raft race, fireworks. Admission to some events. (July, mid-month, weeklong)

LAGRANGE COUNTY 4-H FAIR

NE – LaGrange, County Fairgrounds. (260) 768-4165. 4-H shows and midway. Admission per carload. (July, mid-month for one week)

GREAT MILL RACE

NW – Cutler. Adam's Mill. (765) 463-7893. Boat races every half hour; crafts, displays, mill tours and demonstrations, food. FREE. (July, second Saturday)

JULY (cont.)

STARKE COUNTY 4-H FAIR

NW – Hamlet. Fairgrounds (500N & 600E). (219) 772-9141. Projects, posters, animal shows, livestock sale, talent show, carnival, food, games, demonstrations. FREE. (July, third week)

GAELIC FEST

NW – Valparaiso. Sunset Hill Farm. (219) 465-3586. Irish and Scottish celebration.   Dance, music, food and arts/crafts. Admission. (July, second or third Saturday)

PORTER COUNTY FAIR

NW – Valparaiso. Fairgrounds. **www.portercofair.org**. Expo Center. (July, last part of month)

PIEROGI FESTIVAL

NW – Whiting.   Historic Downtown.   (219) 659-0292.   Slovak and Polish delicacies, music, dancing, parade. FREE. (July, last weekend)

HARRISON COUNTY FAIR

SE – Corydon. County Fairgrounds. Carnival food and rides, livestock shows, animal exhibits, horse racing, grandstand shows, demolition derbies and tractor pulls. (July, end of month, beginning of August for one week)

MADISON REGATTA

SE – Madison. Ohio River. **www.madisonregatta.com**. (812) 265-5000. Races featuring the world's fastest boats-unlimited hydroplanes. Also balloon race, parade, music, fireworks. Some events have admission. (July 4th week)

FLOYD COUNTY FAIR

SE – New Albany. Floyd County Fairgrounds, 2818 Green Valley Road. (812) 948-5470. Carnival and 4-H exhibits (open at 6:00pm daily). Also donkey race, livestock, rodeo and grandstand events. (July, weekend after July 4th for six days)

SCOTT COUNTY 4-H FAIR

SE – Scottsburg, County Fairgrounds. (812) 752-8450. Parade, races, 4-H exhibits, shows, rides and food. (July, mid-month for one week)

LIMESTONE HERITAGE FESTIVAL

SW – Bedford. Brian Lane Way. (800) 798-0969. An important Indiana resource, Bedford stone was used to build the Empire State Building and the Pentagon. Quarry tours, parade, fireworks, sculpture exhibits and competition. No Admission. (July 4th)

RIVERFEST

SW – Evansville. Riverside Drive. (812) 424-2986. Four stages of entertainment, food, carnival, children's activities and contests. (Last weekend July, first week Aug)

THUNDER FESTIVAL

SW – Evansville. Downtown Riverfront. (812) 434-4848 or **www.evvthunderfest.org**. See the world's fastest boat race (Thunder on the Ohio), Blue Angels, parades, carnivals, concerts. Admission. (July, week of July 4th)

VANDERBURGH COUNTY FAIR

SW – Evansville. 4-H Fairgrounds. (812) 868-0636. Exhibits, entertainment, food, rides. Admission. (July, last week)

GIBSON COUNTY FAIR

SW – Princeton. Fairgrounds. **www.gibsoncountyfair.com**. (812) 385-3445. Animals exhibits, tractor pulls, horse shows, live entertainment, kids circus, carnival and demolition derbies. (July, begins Sunday after the 4th for one week)

AUGUST

GLASS FESTIVAL

C – **Elwood**. Callaway Park. (765) 552-0180. Glass factory tours include: Prestige Art Glass, SR 13 (765) 552-0688; Spencers Lapidary (marbles), SR 37 & SR 13 (765) 552-0784; The House of Glass, SR 28 (765) 552-6841. Food, carnival, volksmarch, parade. (August, third weekend)

INDIANA STATE FAIR

C – **Indianapolis**. State Fairgrounds. (317) 927-7500 or **www.indianastatefair.com**. Indiana's best exhibitors, competitors and entertainers are joined by top national entertainment. Blue ribbon agricultural exhibits, top Indiana youth exhibitors. Hours 6 am to late evening. Admission. (August, middle of month for 11 days)

SUMMER HEAT

CE – **Muncie**. County Airport. (765) 284-2700. See 45 hot air balloons rise along with air shows, entertainment. Admission. (August, second weekend, Thursday - Saturday)

WOODLAND INDIANA WAYS

CW – **West Lafayette**. (765) 476-8411. Wigwam Village serves as the backdrop for demonstrations of Indiana crafts, Newfoundland travois dogs and more. 18th century Indiana food available. (August, first Saturday)

GENE STRATTON-PORTER CHAUTAUQUA DAYS

NC – **Rome City**. Sylvan Lake. (260) 854-3790. Tea party, Birthday party in Cabin, lake cruises, tours of GSP's (famous author and nature photographer) lovely home and property, food, entertainment. Admission. (August, first half of month)

POPCORN FESTIVAL

NC – Van Buren. Downtown. (765) 934-4888. 25¢ popcorn, popcorn goodies, parade, entertainment, children's activities, cruise-in, line dancing. FREE. (August, second weekend)

WESTERN DAYS

NE – Andrews. Downtown. (260) 786-3848. Dress for the Old West with pioneer games for kids, chuck wagon meals, Nashville entertainment, parade. FREE. (August, second weekend)

WHEELS OF YESTERYEAR ANTIQUE POWER SHOW & PIONEER FESTIVAL

NE – Bluffton. (260) 565-3217. Pre-1840 encampment, pioneer crafts, antique tractor and engine show. Tractor pulls, flea market and auction. FREE. (August)

INDIAN POW-WOW

NE – Columbia City. Mihsihkinaahkwa Pow Wow Morsches Park. (260) 982-7172. Authentic Native American music and dance. Food (buffalo), storytelling, traditional crafts, and historical language. Admission. (August, second weekend)

FT. WAYNE RAILROAD HISTORICAL OPEN HOUSE

NE – New Haven. 15808 Edgerton Rd. (260) 493-0765. Home to steam locomotive 765, a smaller switching steam locomotive, two wooden cabooses, a 200-ton wrecker, a diesel locomotive and other historic railroad equipment. You can tour the facility and talk to the people who maintain and operate this historic rail equipment, sit in the engineer's seat of a 400-ton iron horse and get a conductor's eye view from a 100-year-old caboose. Take a 20-minute ride in a vintage caboose. (August)

PICKLE FEST

NE – St. Joe. (260) 337-5461 or **www.stjoepicklefest.com**. Pickle Derby, Pickle People Contest, variety of children's activities (including a large petting zoo), great entertainment, and a huge craft tent. (August, second full weekend)

AUGUST (cont.)

LAKE COUNTY FAIR

NW – Crown Point. www.crownpoint.net. As Indiana's largest county fair, the Lake County Fair proudly hosts 4-H displays, agricultural showcases, entertainment events, food and craft booths. (August, beginning first Friday for 9 days)

POTATO FEST

NW – Medaryville. Downtown. (219) 843-3371. Spuds with every imaginable topping, curly fries, numerous potato creations. FREE. (August, mid-month weekend)

STRASSENFEST

SW – Jasper. Downtown. (812) 482-6866 or (800) 968-4578. **www.jasperstrassenfest.org**. German heritage with music, food, talent show. FREE. (August, first weekend)

WATERMELON FESTIVAL

SW – Owensville. Downtown. **www.gibsoncountyin.org**. (812) 729-7777. All you can eat plus other foods, parade and contests. FREE. (August, first weekend)

SCHWEIZER FEST

SW – Tell City, Hall Park. (812) 547-2385. Swiss-German heritage celebration offering free entertainment, authentic food, rides and market. FREE. (August, begins first Friday for 10 days)

WATERMELON FESTIVAL

SW – Vincennes. Downtown. (812) 882-6440. Free watermelon, food sidewalk sales, sports competition, games pageants, historic site tours. (August, first weekend)

SEPTEMBER

INDIAN POW-WOWS

Authentic Native American dance & music. Food, fry bread, buffalo. Storytelling. Traditional arts, clothing, language & history.

- ❑ **CW – Attica**. Potawatomi Festival. Wabash riverfront. (765) 762-3340. (Third weekend)
- ❑ **SW – Evansville**. Native American Days. Angel Mounds. (812) 853-3956. Admission. (Last weekend)

LITTLE ITALY FESTIVAL

CW – Clinton. Water Street. (765) 832-6606. Italian music and authentic food. Spaghetti-eating contest, grape stomping. FREE. (Labor Day Weekend)

LABOR DAY BREAKOUT

CW – Crawfordsville. Old Jail Museum. (800) 866-3973. See the only rotary jail built in Indiana (cells turn every half hour). Music, entertainment, children's events, free refreshments. No Admission. (Labor Day)

ETHNIC FESTIVAL

CW – Terre Haute. Fairbanks Park. (812) 234-5555. Sample the world through ethnic displays, costumes, music, dance and foods. FREE. (September, fourth Saturday)

GLOBAL FEST

CW – West Lafayette. Morton community Center. (765) 775-5120. Celebrate the city's many cultures with international foods, cultural displays, dance, music. FREE. (Labor Day Weekend)

FAIRMONT MUSEUM DAYS FESTIVAL

NC – Fairmount. Main Street. (765) 948-4555 or **www.jamesdeanartifacts.com**. Tour Fairmount Historical Museum/James Dean Museum. Parade, look-alike contest, entertainment with 50's music, dance contest, all James Dean movies playing, plus recognition of hometowner, Jim Davis' "Garfield" series. FREE. (September, last weekend)

SEPTEMBER (cont.)

BLUEBERRY FESTIVAL

NC – Plymouth. Marshall County. Centennial Park. (888) 936-5020 or **www.blueberryfestival.org**. Largest 3 day festival in Indiana with blueberry treats like milkshakes, pie and ice cream. Parade, circus, fireworks, fair food. FREE. (Labor Day Weekend)

AUBURN-CORD DUESENBERG FESTIVAL

NE – Auburn. (260) 925-3600 or **www.acdfestival.org**. Classic car showcase. Parade of Classics, automotive museums, entertainment and a kids art tent. Admission. (Labor Day Weekend)

MARSHMALLOW FESTIVAL

NE – Ligonier. Main Street. (260) 894-9000 or **www.marshmallowfestival.com**. The country's center for marshmallow making. Bake-off, marshmallow putting contest, games, rides, entertainment, parade, area factory history. FREE. (Labor Day Weekend)

PUMPKIN TRAINS

NE – Wakarusa. Old Railroad. (574) 862-2714. Take a mini train ride to the patch and pick a free pumpkin. Admission. (September / October)

WIZARD OF OZ FESTIVAL

NW – Chesterton. Downtown. (219) 926-5513. Oz Fantasy Museum tours, look-alike contests, meet some of the actual MGM Munchkins. FREE. (September, third weekend)

STEAM & POWER SHOW

NW – Hesston. Steam Museum. (219) 872-5055. Rated Top 10 Festival. Steam train rides across 155 scenic acres. Also see restored steam power plant, sawmill, antique engines, tractors. Admission. (Labor Day Weekend)

OKTOBERFEST

NW – Michigan City. Lakefront. (219) 874-8927. International food, artistry, entertainment like dancing and music, rides. Admission. (Labor Day Weekend)

DAN PATCH DAYS

NW – Oxford. Rommel Park. (765) 385-2251. Rodeo, draft horse pull, Dan Patch memorabilia (famous pacer horse), parade, entertainment, bingo. Admission. (September, first weekend after Labor Day)

BALLOONFEST

NW – Valparaiso. Porter county Fairgrounds. (219) 464-8332. 20 some balloons with launch and glows, food, souvenirs. Admission. (September, first weekend after Labor Day)

POPCORN FESTIVAL

NW – Valparaiso. Downtown. **www.popcornfest.org**. (219) 464-8332. In honor of the late Orville Redenbacher and his origin from this town. Popcorn parade, hot air balloon show, children's play areas, food, live entertainment. FREE. (September, first weekend after Labor Day)

FOSSIL FEST

SE – Clarksville. Falls of the Ohio State Park. (812) 280-9970. Special exhibits, guest speakers, fossil & mineral dealers, children's activity area and fossil collection piles donated by Liter's Quarry. (September, third weekend)

AVIATION AWARENESS DAYS

SE – Salem. Municipal Airport. (812) 755-4541. Hot air balloon race, parachutists, aircraft. Entertainment, breakfast and lunch served. FREE. (Labor Day Weekend)

PUMPKIN SHOW

SE – Versailles. Courthouse Square. (812) 689-6188. Carnival, concessions, contest, entertainment, parade. Giant pumpkin weighing & pumpkin foods. FREE. (September, last weekend)

SEPTEMBER (cont.)

PUMPKIN FESTIVAL

SW – French Lick. Downtown, Maple St & SR56. (812) 936-2137. Big Pumpkin Parade, carnival, food. FREE. (September, last week to beginning of October)

PERSIMMON FESTIVAL

SW – Mitchell. Main Street. (800) 580-1985. Persimmon pudding and other novelty persimmon dishes plus bake-off. Parade, carnival, entertainment. FREE. (September, last full week)

TURKEY TROT FESTIVAL

SW – Montgomery, Ruritan Park, north of Hwy. 50. (812) 254-4544. The nationally known event features many turkey races, live entertainment, bingo, greased pig contests, and food. (September, first long weekend)

SEPTEMBER / OCTOBER

HARVEST FESTIVALS

Horses plow fields, antique tractors, chuckwagon-style dinner, corn shredding, tractor pull, hayrides, corn shucking competition and straw baling.

- ❑ **C – Fishers**. Agricultural Fair. Conner Prairie. (800) 966-1836. Admission. (Last weekend in September)
- ❑ **CW – Rockville**. Steam Harvest Days. Billie Creek Village. (765) 569-3430 or **www.billiecreek.org**. Admission. (Labor Day Weekend)
- ❑ **NW – Idaville**, Millers Tree Farm, 11197 E. 700 St. (574) 278-7315. Weekday School Field Trip Programs, too. Admission. (last weekend in September, every weekend in October)
- ❑ **NW – Valparaiso**, Sunset Farm Hill County Park. (219) 462-3965
- ❑ **NW – Wanatah**. Scarecrow Festival. US 421 & US 30. (219) 733-2183. FREE. (September, fourth weekend)

FALL PLAYLANDS

Corn Mazes, Hayrides, Petting Animals, Pick-a-Pumpkin patches, Scarecrows, Painted Pumpkins, Pumpkin Carving Contests, refreshments and entertainment.

- ❏ **C – Indianapolis.** Waterman's Farm Market. 7010 E. Raymond St. Admission. (317) 357-2989. (October, daily)
- ❏ **CE – Bryant.** Scarecrow Contest. Bearcreek Farms. (800) 288-7630 or **www.bearcreekfarms.com.** (first half of October)
- ❏ **CE – Cambridge City.** Dougherty Orchards. (765) 478-5198 or **www.doughertyorchards.com.** Also, Apple House Tours. Admission. (September – December, Daily)
- ❏ **NC – Goshen.** Kercher's Sunrise Orchards. CR 38. (574) 533-6311. (Mid-September to Mid-October)
- ❏ **NC – Millersburg.** Indiana Maze Plex. 69623 SR 13. (574) 642-5111. (August – October)
- ❏ **NC - Peru.** Tate Orchard / Apple Dumpling Inn. (765) 985-2467
- ❏ **NE - Ligonier.** Pumpkin Fantasyland. Fashion Farm, 1680 Lincolnway West. (800) 254-8090. (October)
- ❏ **NW – Hobart.** County Line Orchard. (219) 947-4477. (October)
- ❏ **SE – Starlight.** Joe Huber Family Farm & Restaurant. 2421 Scottsville Road (I – 64 East to Exit 119). (877) JOE HUBERS or **www.joehubers.com.** Also apple orchard in September (wagon ride to orchard for picking). (September / October)

APPLE FESTIVALS

Apple peeling and pie-eating contests, apple foods demos, apple foods-pies, donuts, cider, butter. Carnival.

- ❏ **C – Danville.** Heartland Apple Festival, Beasley's Orchard. (317) 745-4876 or **www.beasleysorchard.com.** Farming animal shows, puppets, storytelling. $5.00 per vehicle. (October, first and second weekend)
- ❏ **C - Pendleton.** Grabow's Orchard. 6397 SR 13 off I-69. (888) 534-3225. Raspberries too! (September, last Saturday)

APPLE FESTIVALS - September / October (cont.)

APPLE FESTIVALS - September / October (cont.)

- ❑ **C – Sheridan**. Stuckey Farm Market, (2 ½ miles north of SR32 on County Line Rd). (317) 769-4172. FREE. (June-November, daily except Sunday)
- ❑ **CE – Bryant**. Bearcreek Farms. (800) 288-7630 or **www.bearcreekfarms.com**.
- ❑ **CE – Cambridge City**. Dougherty Orchard. 1117 Dougherty Road off US 40. **www.doughertyorchards.com**. (765) 478-5198 or Apple jellies, petting zoo, aviary. Daily. (July – December)
- ❑ **NC - Nappanee**. (800) 517-9739. 600 lb. Apple pie. (September, third weekend)
- ❑ **NC – Peru**. Tate Orchard. (765) 985-2467. Apples and dumplings.
- ❑ **NW – Hobart**. County Line Orchard. (219) 947-4477. (third Saturday in September)
- ❑ **NW – Laporte**. Garwood Orchards. (219) 362-4385. (September, mid-month Saturday)
- ❑ **SE – Batesville**. Liberty Park. (812) 933-6103. FREE. (September, last weekend)
- ❑ **SE – Starlight**. Stumler Orchard., 10924 St. John's Road. (812) 923-3832. Hayrides to the pumpkin patch. FREE. (October, first weekend)
- ❑ **SW – Chrisney**. (812) 359-4789. (October, first weekend)

OKTOBERFEST

German music and dance, food, parade, carnival and hayrides.

- ❑ **SW – Huntingburg**. Herbstfest. City Park at First & Cherry Streets. (812) 683-5699. (October, first long weekend)
- ❑ **SW– New Harmony**. Kunstfest. (800) 231-2168. Petting zoo, wagon rides, general store, historic homes to tour. FREE, some fees for historic tours. (September, two weekends after Labor Day)

OCTOBER

INDIAN POW WOW

C – Anderson. Indian Trails Festival. Riverfront. (765) 642-7600. Authentic music, dance, food (fry bread, buffalo), storytelling, art and history. FREE. (October, second weekend)

RILEY FESTIVAL

C – Greenfield. Downtown. (317) 462-2141. Commemorate James Whitcomb Riley's birthday. Parades, entertainment, pumpkin contest, food. FREE. (October, first Thursday – Sunday)

PUMPKIN PATCH TRAIN

CE – Knightstown. Carthage, Knightstown and Shirley Railroad Train. (765) 345-5561. The train stops at a field of pumpkins where the kids can get off the train and find just the right pumpkin for themselves, which they must carry back to the train. Advance reservations. Train admission fees. (October, each weekend).

PARKE COUNTY COVERED BRIDGE FESTIVAL

CW – Ten days in the middle of October. County celebrates Indiana's historic past with 32 Historic Covered Bridges. Hours: 9:00am-6:00pm. FREE. **www.coveredbridges.com.**

- ❑ **Rockville** – Headquarters. Sample cooking and crafts. Bus tours.
- ❑ **Billie Creek Village** – America's largest gathering of turn-of-the-century craftsmen. 3 bridges, entertainment, horse-pulled wagon rides, authentic foods and costumes. Admission. BLACK ROUTE.
- ❑ **Bridgeton** – 245-foot double-span covered bridge above the dam, waterfall near a working gristmill. Weaver, crafters, food. RED ROUTE.
- ❑ **Mansfield** – Historic Village, 1820's water-powered grist mill, 1867 covered bridge. BLACK ROUTE.

PARKE COUNTY COVERED BRIDGE FESTIVAL–October (cont.)

- ❑ **Mecca** – 2 historic schoolhouses, covered bridge, 1800's outdoor metal jail, old clay tile factory, crafts, foods, and dancing on the bridge. BROWN ROUTE & RED ROUTE.
- ❑ **Montezuma** – Historic river town and home of the Wabash-Erie Canal bed, Aztec trading post, hog roast, hayrides, trail rides.
- ❑ **Rosedale** – Potato fields, antique equipment. RED ROUTE.
- ❑ **Tangier** – 5 covered bridges, serve Tangier's famous "buried roast beef". BLUE & YELLOW ROUTE.

LEWIS AND CLARK RIVER FESTIVAL

SE – Clarksville, Falls of the Ohio State Park, George Rogers Clark Homesite. (812) 283-4999 or **www.fallsoftheohio.org**. Re-enactors portray William Clark, Meriwether Lewis and George Rogers Clark, and the Lewis and Clark "Corps of Discovery" expedition. They left Mill Creek in Clarksville in 1803 to discover the West. Children's games, craft demos and book signings. (October, last weekend)

NOVEMBER / DECEMBER

WINTER WONDERLAND TRAIN

NE – Wakarusa. Old Wakarusa Railroad. (574) 862-2714. Diesel train (mini) ride through decorated trees, bridges, buildings and tunnels with holiday music throughout. 30 minute rides. Dress warmly. (Thanksgiving – first weekend in January)

FESTIVAL OF GINGERBREAD

NE – Fort Wayne. Old City Hall Historical Museum. (260) 426-2882. Creations of fantasy gingerbread houses on display. (Children's to Professional categories) Admission. (Thanksgiving through mid-December)

A COURTYARD CHRISTMAS

SE – Scottsburg. Scott County Courthouse Courtyard. (812) 752-4343. 700 plus luminaries glowing, carriage rides, food, entertainment, parade with Santa, children's games and carolers. FREE. (Saturday after Thanksgiving)

HOLIDAY LIGHTS

SE – Starlight. Joe Huber Family Farm and Restaurant. (812) 923-5255 or **www.joehuber.com**. Holiday entertainment by Music Theatre Louisville. A holiday celebration as grandmother remembers the true meaning of Christmas with help from her grandchildren and a couple of jovial Christmas fairies. Ticket price includes Huber's famous holiday dinner buffet and show. Adults $34.95, Children (4-10) $14.95. Dinner 6:30, Show 7:30pm. (Thanksgiving weekend thru mid-December)

FESTIVAL OF LIGHTS

Lighted roadways or walkways. Entertainment. Carolers. Santa. Themed with characters and historical events. (Evenings beginning the weekend of Thanksgiving through December unless noted otherwise)

- ❑   **C – Columbus**. Mill Race Park. (800) 468-6564 or **www.columbus.in.us**. Over 1.5 million lights. Admission.
- ❑   **C – Fishers**. Conner Prairie by Candlelight. (800) 966-1836 or **www.connerprairie.org**. Walk-thru a holiday village 1836 and Festival of Gingerbread display. Admission/Reservations. (December, Wednesday-Sunday evenings)
- ❑   **C – Indianapolis**. Christmas at the Zoo. Indianapolis Zoo. (317) 630-2001. 700,000 lights and 180 displays. Train & Trolley Rides. Admission.
- ❑   **CE – Metamora**. Old Fashioned Christmas Walk. (765) 647-6512. Luminaries along roads and canal banks. FREE
- ❑   **CE – Muncie**. Minnetrista Cultural Center & Gardens. (765) 282-4848 or **www.mccoak.org**.
- ❑   **CE – Parker City**. Holiday House of Lights, ME's Zoo. (765) 468-8559.

FESTIVAL OF LIGHTS – November / December (cont.)

- ☐ **NC – Marion**. International Walkway of Lights, Riverwalk. (800) 662-9474. Walk or drive, Gift shop. Daily. FREE.
- ☐ **NW – Valparaiso**. Sunset Hill Farm County Park, Hwy. 6. (219) 465-3586. (November)
- ☐ **SE – Rising Sun**. Holiday Winter Walk. Riverfront. (888) RSNG SUN. Turn of the century light display on the riverfront, Santa's Castle and horse-drawn carriage. FREE. (December, first weekend)
- ☐ **SW – Evansville**. Fantasy of Lights. Garvin Park. (812)474-2348. Admission.
- ☐ **SW – Santa Claus**. (812) 937-2848. Tour thru Christmas Lake Village.

FESTIVAL OF TREES

Beautifully decorated trees for sale to benefit charity. Gift shops. Entertainment. (End of November)

- ☐ **C– Anderson**. Paramount Theatre. (765) 642-1234. Admission. (December, first week)
- ☐ **NE – Fort Wayne**. Embassy Theatre. (260) 424-4071. Admission.

DECEMBER

HOLIDAY OPEN HOUSES

Holiday decorated historic homes with costumed interpreters and special music and refreshments.

- ☐ **C – Anderson**. Gruenewalt House. (765) 646-5771. (December, first weekend)
- ☐ **C – Indianapolis**. Pres. Benjamin Harrison Home. (317) 631-1888. Family Christmas -meet President Harrison and the household staff in various rooms through the house. Admission. (mid-December Saturday)

❑ **CE – Cambridge City.** Family Christmas Festival at Huddleston Farmhouse Inn. (765) 478-3172. (Early to mid-December)

❑ **CE – Richmond.** Christmas at Wayne County Museum. (765) 962-5756. (December, first Sunday)

❑ **CW – Lafayette.** Victorian Christmas Tour of Fowler House, Tippecanoe County Museum. (765) 476-8402 or **www.tcha.mus.in.us**

❑ **NC – Bristol.** A Victorian Christmas Celebration. Elkhart County Museum. (574) 848-4322. Many Victorian Christmas characters and meal. Admission. (December, first or second weekend)

❑ **NC– Elkhart.** Ruthmere Museum. (800) 517-9737. (December, first Saturday)

❑ **NC – Kokomo.** Christmas at the Seiberling Mansion. (765) 452-4314. Admission. (Thanksgiving weekend to third week of December)

❑ **NC – South Bend.** Christmas at Copshaholm. (574) 235-9664. Admission. (Thanksgiving weekend to week after New Years)

❑ **NE – Geneva.** Limberlost State Historic Site. (260) 368-7428. (December, second weekend)

❑ **NE – Huntington.** Christmas at the Forks. (260) 356-1903. (December, first weekend)

❑ **NW – Lowell.** Christmas at Buckley Homestead. (219) 696-6769. (December, first weekend)

❑ **NW – Michigan City.** Christmas at Barker Mansion, 631 Washington St. (219) 873-1520. Admission. (first Saturday in December to mid-January)

❑ **NW – Porter.** Christmas in the Dunes. Chellberg Farm & Bailly Homestead. (219) 926-7561. (December, second Sunday)

❑ **SE – Aurora.** Hillforest Mansion, 213 Fifth St.. (812) 926-0087 or **www.dearborncounty.org**. Victorian Christmas. Admission. (December, first two weekends)

❑ **SE – Madison.** Nights Before Christmas in Historic District. (812) 265-2956. Admission. (Thanksgiving weekend to first weekend in December)

HOLIDAY OPEN HOUSES – December (cont.)

- ❑ **SE – Vevay.** Over the River and Through the Woods, Downtown. (800) HELLO-VV. Admission. (December, first weekend)
- ❑ **SW – Boonville.** (812) 897-3100. Christmas in Boon Village and at the Warrick County Museum, decorated.
- ❑ **SW – Evansville.** Rietz Home. (812) 426-1871. (Thanksgiving week to Christmas week, daily except Monday)
- ❑ **SW – Gentryville.** Christmas through the Ages at Col. William Jones State Historic Site. (812) 937-2802. (December, second weekend)
- ❑ **SW – New Harmony.** (812) 682-4488. Historic homes / village and museum. Admission. (December, first Saturday)

CIRCLE OF LIGHTS

C – Indianapolis. Monument Circle. (317) 237-2222. Lighting of the "World's Largest Christmas Tree" plus singing from the Indianapolis Children's Choir. FREE. (December, mid-month thru first week of Jan.)

POLAR BEAR EXPRESS

C – Noblesville. Indiana Transportation Museum. (317) 773-6000. Train tickets include a reading and visual presentation of the popular story "The Polar Express", train ride and snacks. Admission and reservations. (December, first two weekends)

CHRISTMAS TRAIN

CE – Connersville. Whitewater Valley Railroad. (765) 825-2054 or **www.whitewatervalleyrr.org**. Special holiday shopping excursions to Metamora. Santa Claus rides many of these trains to add to the holiday fun. Early reservations are highly recommended. Admission $8.00-$16.00. (Friday nights, Saturday and Sunday afternoons for the three weekends following Thanksgiving)

PARKE COUNTY COVERED BRIDGE CHRISTMAS

CW – Rockville. Parke County Fairgrounds & other locations. (765) 569-5226. Travel through historic covered bridges and villages decorated for the holidays. Shopping, food. FREE. (December, first full weekend)

CHRISTMAS WALK

CW – Terre Haute. Fowler Park Pioneer Log Village. (812) 462-3392. Historic village streets decorated for the holidays, dulcimer music, refreshments. Dress warmly, bring a flashlight. FREE. (December, first weekend)

LIVE NATIVITY SCENE

NE – Shipshewana. Downtown. **www.shipshewana.com**. (260) 768-4163 or Costumed interpreters re-enact and celebrate the birth of Christ. Live animals and caroling too. FREE. (December, third weekend)

LIVE NATIVITY

NW – Valparaiso. Courthouse. (219) 464-8332. Live Nativity with animals. Caroling, carriage rides, refreshments, pictures with Santa. FREE. (December, first Saturday)

SANTA CLAUS POST OFFICE

SW – Santa Claus. Hwy 162 and 245. (812) 937-4469. Nation's only post office with a "Santa Claus" postmark. (December, daily except Sunday)

NEW YEAR'S EVE CELEBRATION

Non-alcoholic party includes music, dance, clowns, storytellers, magicians, juggling and fireworks.

- ❑ **NC – Elkhart**. FamilyFest. (800) 262-8161. Admission.
- ❑ **SW – Evansville**. First Night. (812) 422-2111. Admission.

YEAR LONG

PIONEER DAYS / ENCAMPMENTS

Early 1800's frontier life. Period costumed townsfolk, soldiers, Native Americans. See fur trading posts, kids' infantry, barber shop medicine, and old-fashioned games. Demonstrations of spinning, broom making, dancing, weaving, woodcarving, blacksmiths and tomahawk throwing. Open hearth cooking with period foods for sale like kettle popcorn and chips, cider, stew, barbecue, buffalo burgers, dumplings, apple butter, ham & beans, birch tea and Indian fry bread.

APRIL

MOUNTAIN MEN RENDEZVOUS

CW – **Bridgeton**. (765) 548-2136. **www.coveredbridges.com** FREE. (April)

REDBUD TRAIL RENDEZVOUS

NC – **Rochester**. Fulton County Historical Society Grounds. (574) 223-4436. Admission. (April)

MAY

FESTIVAL OF THE WHIPPOORWILL MOON

NE – **Huntington**. Forks of the Wabash Park. (260) 356-1903. (May, first weekend)

WESSELMAN WOODS NATURE PRESERVE

SW – **Evansville**. (812) 479-0771. (May, third weekend)

SPIRIT OF VINCENNES RENDEZVOUS

SW – **Vincennes**. French Commons. (812) 882-7079. Battlefield activities of George Rogers Clark. Admission. (Memorial Day weekend)

JUNE

CIVIL WAR DAYS

CW – **Rockville**. Billie Creek Village. (765) 569-3430 or **www.billiecreek.org**. Indiana's largest Civil War reenactment with tractor shuttle from Rockville. Admission. (June, second weekend)

FEAST OF THE WILD ROSE MOON

NC – **Middlebury**. Loveway Horseback Riding Facility. (574) 293-4640. Step back in time as you visit buckskinners and fur traders from the French and Indian War era. Admission. (June, first weekend)

JULY

HOOSIER HISTORY FEST

C – **Indianapolis**. Indiana Historical Society. (317) 232-1882 or **www.indianahistory.org/fest**. Enjoy family activities, historical re-enactors, encampments, exhibitions, music and more while you learn about Indiana's fascinating history. FREE. (July, last Saturday)

OLD CAPITOL DAYS

SE - **Corydon**. First State Office Building lawn. (812) 738-4890. Living history encampments covering periods from 1756-1812. Demonstrations and storytelling each day. FREE. (July, weekend after the 4th)

MORGAN'S RAID, SCOTT COUNTY

SE – **Lexington**, Township Park. (812) 752-7270. (July, weekend after the 4th).

AUGUST

SKINNER FARM MUSEUM & VILLAGE

CW – **Perrysville**. SR32W. (765) 793-4079. Admission. (August, third weekend)

AUGUST (cont.)

DAVID ROGERS DAY

NE – LaGrange. David Rogers Park. (260) 463-7825. Admission. (August, late in the month)

HAMLET FESTIVAL & RENDEZVOUS

NW – Hamlet. 4-H County Fairgrounds. (574) 586-2105. FREE. (August, third weekend).

SEPTEMBER

HERITAGE DAYS

C - Indianapolis. Robin Run Village. (317) 293-5500. FREE. (September, third weekend)

CIVIL WAR ENCAMPMENT

CE – Cambridge City. Huddleston Farmhouse Inn. (765) 478-3172. Admission. (Weekend after Labor Day)

WAYNE COUNTY HISTORICAL MUSEUM

CE – Richmond. (765) 962-5756. Admission. (September, second weekend)

BACK TO THE DAYS OF KOSCIUSZKO

NC – Warsaw. Lucerne Park. (574) 267-2012. Admission. (September, last weekend)

HERITAGE FESTIVAL

NE – Berne. Swiss Heritage Village. (260) 589-8007 or **www.bernein.com/heritagedays.htm**. Pioneer games, storytelling, scarecrow contest, apple cider press, village tours, pioneer music and food, Native American dancing. Admission. (September, second weekend)

JOHNNY APPLESEED FESTIVAL

NE – Fort Wayne. Johnny Appleseed Park. (260) 497-6000. Celebrate the life and times of John Chapman. 100,000 attendance. (September, third weekend)

FORKS OF THE WABASH PIONEER FESTIVAL

NE – Huntington. Hiers Park. (800) 848-4282. Admission. (September, third or fourth weekend)

STONE'S TRACE PIONEER FESTIVAL

NE – Ligonier. (888) 417-3562. Pony cart rides, tour of Stone's Tavern, pioneer music, tomahawk throwing, circuit riding preacher, women's skillet throw, log splitting, primitive muzzle loading demos, food and entertainment. Admission. (September, weekend after Labor Day)

BUCKSKINNERS RENDEZVOUS

NW – Cutler. Adams Mill. (765) 463-7893. Admission. (September, last Saturday)

DUNELAND HARVEST FESTIVAL

NW – Porter. Chellberg Farm & Bailly Homestead. (219) 926-7561. FREE. (September, third weekend)

OLD SETTLERS DAYS

SE – Salem. Steven's Memorial Museum. (812) 883-4500. (September, mid-month)

COUNCIL GROUND GATHERING

SW – Vincennes. Indiana Territory State Historic Site. (812) 882-7422. FREE. (Labor Day weekend)

OCTOBER

CIVIL WAR DAYS & LIVING HISTORY

CE – Hartford City. SR 26. (765) 348-1905. Also tour a medical training school. Admission. (October, second weekend)

OCTOBER (cont.)

CANAL DAYS & TRADERS RENDEZVOUS

CE – Metamora. (765) 647-2194 or **www.metamora.com**. Little shops plus historical vendors and re-enactors. FREE. (October, first weekend)

PIONEER DAYS

CW – Terre Haute.   Fowler Park.   (812) 462-3391. FREE. (October, first weekend)

FEAST OF THE HUNTER'S MOON

CW – West Lafayette. Fort Quiatenon Historic Park. South River Road. (765) 476-8402 or **www.tcha.mus.in.us/feast.htm**. Re-creation of life at this 18th century French trading post. Admission. (October, second weekend)

MISSISSINEWA 1812

NC – Marion. Battlefield. (800) 822-1812. Largest War of 1812 living history event in the U.S. with average attendance of 30,000. Admission. (October, end of first full week)

BUCKLEY HOMESTEAD DAYS

NW – Lowell. (219) 696-0769. Admission. (October, first weekend)

AUTUMN ON THE RIVER

SE – Bethlehem. Town Commons. (812) 256-6111. Recreation of founding of Bethlehem in 1812. Taste this town's famous steamboat stew and flatboat bean soup. FREE. (October, third weekend)

FT. VALLONIA DAYS

SE – Vallonia. (888) 524-1914. Reconstructed fort/tepees. FREE (October, third weekend)

Master
Index

**WEST CLINTON
MENNONITE CHURCH**

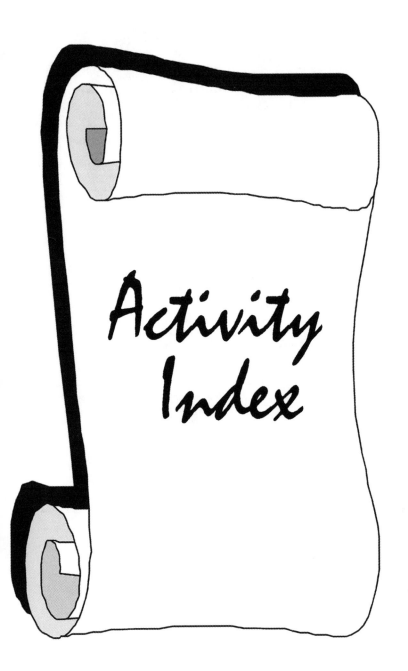

Index by Activity *(Area, City, Place/Event Name, Page)*

AMUSEMENTS

ANIMALS & FARMS

INDIANA HISTORY

Index by Activity *(Area, City, Place/Event Name, Page)*

Index by Activity *(Area, City, Place/Event Name, Page)*

Index by Activity *(Area, City, Place/Event Name, Page)*

Index by Activity *(Area, City, Place/Event Name, Page)*

NOTES

NOTES

<u>NOTES</u>

NOTES

GROUP DISCOUNTS & FUNDRAISING OPPORTUNITIES!

We're excited to introduce our books to your group! These guides for parents, grandparents, teachers and visitors are great tools to help you discover hundreds of fun places to visit. Our titles are great resources for all the wonderful places to travel either locally or across the region.

We are two parents who have researched, written and published these books. We have spent thousands of hours collecting information and *personally traveled over 20,000 miles* visiting all of the most unique places listed in our guides. The books are kid-tested and the descriptions include great hints on what kids like best!

Please consider the following Group Purchase options: *For the latest information, visit our website:* **www.kidslovepublications.com**

❑ **Group Discount/Fundraising** – Purchase books at the discount price of $2.95 off the suggested retail price for members/friends. <u>Minimum order is ten books.</u> You may mix titles to reach the minimum order. Greater discounts (~35%) are available for fundraisers. <u>Minimum order is thirty books.</u> Call for details.

❑ **Available for Interview/Speaking** – The authors have a treasure bag full of souvenirs from favorite places. We'd love to share ideas on planning fun trips to take children while exploring your home state. The authors are available, by appointment, *(based on availability)* at (614) 792-6451. The minimum guaranteed order is: 30 books in Ohio, 50 books for other states. There is no additional fee involved.

<u>**Call us soon at (614) 792-6451 to make arrangements**</u>!
Happy Exploring!

YOUR FAMILY MEMORIES!

Now that you've created memories with your family,

it's time to keepsake them by scrapbooking

in this unique, family-friendly way!

Check Out These Unique Features:

* **The Book That Shrinks As It Grows!** - Specially designed pages can be removed as you add
  pictures to your book. This keeps your unique travel journal from becoming too thick to use.

* **Write Your Own Book** - The travel journal is designed to get you started and help you remember
  those great family fun times!

* **Design Your Own Book** - Most illustrations and picture frames are designed to encourage kids to
  color them.

* **Unique Chapter Names** - help you <u>simply</u> categorize your family travel memories.

* **Acid Free Paper** - was used to print your book to keep your photos safe for a lifetime!

Writing Your Own Family Travel Book is This Easy...

Step 1 - Select, Cut and Paste Your Favorite Travel Photos

Step 2 - Color the Fun Theme Picture Frames

Step 3 - Write about Your Travel Stories in the Journal (We get you started...)

Step 4 - Specially Designed Pages are removed to reduce thickness as you add photos

Create Your Family Travel Book Today!

Visit your local retailer,

use the order form in the back of this book,

or our website: www.kidslovepublications.com

Attention Parents:

All titles are "Kid Tested". *The authors and kids personally visited all of the most unique places* and wrote the books with warmth and excitement from a parent's perspective. Find tried and true places that children will enjoy. No more boring trips! Listings provide: Names, addresses, telephone numbers, websites, directions, and descriptions. All books include a bonus chapter listing state-wide kid-friendly Seasonal & Special Events!

❑ **KIDS LOVE INDIANA** - Discover places where you can "co-star" in a cartoon or climb a giant sand dune. Over 500 listings in one book about Indiana travel. 8 geographical zones, 213 pages.

❑ **KIDS LOVE KENTUCKY** - Discover places from Boone to Burgoo, from Caves to Corvettes, and from Lincoln to the Lands of Horses. Over 500 listings in one book about Kentucky travel. 6 geographic zones. 224 pages.

❑ **KIDS LOVE MICHIGAN** - Discover places where you can "race" over giant sand dunes, climb aboard a lighthouse "ship", eat at the world's largest breakfast table, or watch yummy foods being made. Almost 600 listings in one book about Michigan travel. 8 geographical zones, 237 pages.

❑ **KIDS LOVE OHIO** - Discover places like hidden castles and whistle factories. Almost 1000 listings in one book about Ohio travel. 9 geographical zones, 257 pages.

❑ **KIDS LOVE PENNSYLVANIA** - Explore places where you can "discover" oil and coal, meet Ben Franklin, or watch you favorite toys and delicious, fresh snacks being made. Over 900 listings in one book about Pennsylvania travel. 9 geographical zones, 268 pages.

❑ **KIDS LOVE THE VIRGINIAS** – Discover where ponies swim and dolphins dance, dig into archaeology and living history, or be dazzled by record-breaking and natural bridges. Over 900 listings in one book about Virginia & West Virginia travel. 8 geographical zones, 262 pages.

❑ **KIDS LOVE TRAVEL MEMORIES!** – The Perfect Travel Journal & Scrapbook Companion. – See display page (or our website) to learn more about the features of this unique book.

ORDER FORM

KIDS LOVE PUBLICATIONS

7438 Sawmill Road, # 500
Columbus, OH 43235
(614) 792-6451
Visit our website: **www.kidslovepublications.com**

#	Title		Price	Total
	Kids Love Michigan		$12.95	
	Kids Love Pennsylvania		$12.95	
	Kids Love Indiana		$13.95	
	Kids Love Ohio		$13.95	
	Kids Love Kentucky		$13.95	
	Kids Love the Virginias		$13.95	
	Kids Love Travel Memories!		$14.95	
	COMBO PRICING* - *Indicate Titles Above*			
	Combo #2 - Any 2 Titles*		$22.95	
	Combo #3 - Any 3 Titles*		$32.95	
	Combo #4 - Any 4 Titles*		$41.95	
			Subtotal	
*Note: All combo pricing is for **different titles only.** For multiple copies (10+) of one title, please call or visit our website for volume pricing information.	*(Ohio Residents Only)*	5.75% Sales Tax		
	$2.00 first book $1.00 each additional	Shipping		
		TOTAL		

[] Master Card   [] Visa

Account Number _ _ _ _ - _ _ _ _ - _ _ _ _ - _ _ _ _
Exp Date: _ _ / _ _ (Month/Year)
Cardholder's Name _____
Signature *(required)* _____

(Please make check or money order payable to: KIDS LOVE PUBLICATIONS)

Name: _____
Address:_____
City:_____ State:_____
Zip:_____ Telephone:_____

All orders are shipped within 2 business days of receipt by US Mail. If you wish to have your books autographed, please include a legible note with the message you'd like written in your book. Your satisfaction is 100% guaranteed or simply return your order for a prompt refund. Thanks for your order. Happy Exploring!

"Where to go?, What to do?, and How much will it cost?", are all questions that they have heard throughout the years from friends and family. These questions became the inspiration that motivated them to research, write and publish the "Kids Love" travel series.

This adventure of writing and publishing family travel books has taken them on a journey of experiences that they never could have imagined. They have appeared as guests on over 100 radio and television shows, had featured articles in statewide newspapers and magazines, spoken to thousands of people at schools and conventions, and write monthly columns in many publications talking about "family friendly" places to travel.

George Zavatsky and Michele (Darrall) Zavatsky were raised in the Midwest and have lived in many different cities. They currently reside in a suburb of Columbus, Ohio. They feel very blessed to be able to create their own career that allows them to research, write and publish a series of best-selling kids' travel books. Besides the wonderful adventure of marriage, they place great importance on being loving parents to Jenny & Daniel.